WHO'S YOUR DADDY?
"Healing the Father Wound"

written by
Waylon Ward
Global Fathering Initiative

Endorsements

❦━━╪━━❦

" **A** s a generation, one of the biggest issues we face is father-lessness. We have a generation of boys, raised by women, who don't know what it is to be a man, husband, or father; and a generation of girls raised without the protection, affirmation, or wholesome affection of a father. In his book, *Who's Your Daddy?*, Waylon Ward tackles these tough issues head on. He outlines the challenges of fatherless families, describes the wounds suffered by fatherless children, and gives hope and encouragement in the steps for healing. I highly recommend this book for those looking to address the issue of fatherlessness in their own lives."

Dr. John A. King
Best-selling Author *It's a Guy Thing:*
Helping Guys Become Men, Husbands, and Fathers

"I am glad Waylon has written about this very important subject. He is passionate and knowledgeable about this issue. He has lived in the aftermath of fatherlessness. He is on a journey of discovery and invites us to join him. I don't mind traveling with a learner. I hope many will catch the vision of restoring the father component to society's basic foundation. Reading this book should make us all hunger for the ultimate Father-son relationship we can have because of Jesus the ultimate Son."

Dudley Hall,
Successful Christian Living Ministries
Author of *Grace Works* and *Men in Their Own Skin*.

"I'm honored to recommend to you Waylon Ward's books on family, fatherhood and raising Godly children. I've known Waylon for many, many years and have come to know him as a man of God who speaks wisdom and truth on a daily basis. If you want to become a better parent to your kids or a better person to those around you, read Waylon's books!"

Dr. Joe White
President, Kanakuk Kamps
Best Selling Author

"It gives me great pleasure to recommend Waylon's books on father-hood. I have spent over twenty-five years in counseling and ministry, and have decided that counseling is really a form of re-parenting a person. This is especially true of the role of the father. We have all been created with a strong need to connect with our Heavenly Father as well as our earthly father. The earthly father is an image of our relationship with our Heavenly Father and if it is dysfunctional, there is usually a concomitant disconnect with our Heavenly Father. Waylon has done a great job in bringing this principle to a concise and accurate study in his books. The "father" concept is founda-tional to our concept of God and of the world. For us individually it is vital to our being able to minister in the way God intended, which is to bring all of us into a relationship with the Father through Jesus Christ. Thanks, Waylon."

Dr. Vernon Brinkley
Light House Christian Fellowship
Prosper, Texas

"Waylon Ward is one of God's special tools to help transform the lives of men in our generation. He has a unique gift-set of *"spiritual fathering"* combined with *"godly wisdom."*

Waylon's ministry has been used of the Lord to touch the lives of thousands of hurting men, and now in the fullness of time, is destined to reach entire nations with this crucial life message.

Global Fathering Initiative [GFI] is a strategic ministry, in the providence of God, whose time has come. Your life will be transformed into the fullness of Christ as you imbibe the life-changing truth of this book."

Mike Downey
Founder & CEO, Strategic Impact

"This book's pinpoint accuracy regarding the issues of fatherhood will empower men to raise healthier children that result in healthy marriages in the future. Waylon's insights are deep and his ministry and multiple books have personally made my marriage richer. I have witnessed the deterioration of true fatherhood roles throughout our country's prisons as well as in our Nation's Armed Services. Every one of the men I have met would be wiser and better equipped after reading this book. Thank you, Waylon, for continuing to awaken fathers to the alarming issues that make America's families so dysfunctional. My wife thanks you and I thank you. This book is a must read."

Jonathan Spinks / CEO
OSU Tour

"Now more than ever our fractured societies are in need of Godly Fathers who will be witnesses to the ends of the earth. Waylon has done a masterful job of helping restore men to their Heavenly Father through the love of Christ and equipping them to become those witnesses around the world.

Global Fathering Initiative is clearly not another "program"; instead it's a movement of men who have experienced a revelation in their relationship with God the Father & are now being mobilized to take the message of Masculine Christ-Centered Fathering to the ends of the Earth."

Chad Doughty
Former Director- Youth with a Mission Finland

"It is a privilege for me to recommend Waylon's seminars and books on fatherhood. I have known Waylon for nearly a decade. He is a dear friend and fellow minister. We have prayed together, wept together and co-counseled others. From one who has served as a pastor and counselor for over 30 years, I can tell you this man has a heart for restoring men to their first and foremost important call: effective fathering. Waylon understands that fathers have an indelible impact on the relationship men and women will enjoy, or conversely, fail to enjoy with their Heavenly Father. He also clearly annunciates the redemption that is in Christ and is able to communicate that hope to the many that are in need of a loving Heavenly Father."

Pastor Randy Foret
Restoration Church
St. Paul, Texas

"Waylon Ward's work on Fathering is exciting and refreshing. Waylon gives an account of serious issues facing our culture. He also defines how those issues are associated to a lack of masculinity in our modern society. This is a brave work that may be applied across cultural lines and has the real potential of making a global impact."

Edward C Walters,
Theophilus Ministries

"To some extent I knew who my father was, that is my earthly father. My idea of Abba Father however, did not seem to match up with the one described in the Bible. How could these two figures be so different and both be called "father"? Waylon showed me how my concept of "fathering" has been damaged, to understand how it wounded me, and how to have hope that my Heavenly Father will truly heal my heart and I will be a better father to my son. We all have a father, but many of us need to know our Daddy. This book makes sense."

John Berry
Businessman, Southlake, Texas

"Waylon has been a good friend and a straight-shooting advisor to me as I try to well raise five sons and nurture and love one wife. I am not afraid of failure, but rather succeeding at things that don't matter. Besides his stellar resume, Waylon has a victorious history of dealing with tough issues personally and has become a man who keenly knows the power of God's own restoration. He is not afraid to tackle, head on, deep and troubling problems faced every day by real men trying to live real lives."

A. C. Tracy Wood III
Businessman, Dallas, Texas

"I know many leaders, but none more dedicated. Waylon is wise and tenacious. His passion is to help men get back to the God ordered task of being Christ-like husbands, fathers and family leaders. Who's Your Daddy? is full of grace to minister strength to men who may have accepted something less than God's best. It is my pleasure to recommend the book and the author to you."

Doyle Welch
Businessman, Southlake, Texas

"I'm so excited about the continued published works of Waylon Ward on the topic of fatherhood. His passion to bring the vital importance of fatherhood to the forefront is critical if we are to reverse and erase the erosion that is plaguing our family structure and our ability to deeply understand our relationship with Jesus Christ. Waylon has truly been anointed to this ministry which is reflected in his Biblically accurate research and documentation. He has a real love of people and a keen understanding of the role men hold in the family structure. If it has Waylon's name on it, I'm reading it!"

Bob Davis
President of CareerSurge

Thank You
to my wife, Lynn,
for her love and patience with me
and, most especially, her belief in me.
Thank you for the hours you spent unselfishly editing this book.
The books I have written would not exist without you.
You are a most precious gift to me from God.

About the Title . . .

"**W**ho's your Daddy?" is a 21st century expression that is sometimes used by a basketball coach taunting a player or by inner city kids harassing one another. But it unsettles our heart when we realize it is a valid question for way too many people. Educators report that more and more children on entrance forms complete the question "Father's Name:" with "I don't have one" or "I don't know." Billboards on the main streets of many American cities advertise DNA testing to prove paternity. The percentage of unwed births is now approaching 33 % of all births in the U.S.

The popular musical comedy "Mama Mia!" tells the story of a young woman who grew up never knowing who her father is. But as her wedding day approaches, she desires to have her father present for her special day. She is able to narrow the prospects down to three possible men whose names she gets from her mother's diary. On Broadway and in the movie it makes a humorous plot, but it is no laughing matter for thousands of children in America.

"Who's your Daddy?" is the question of our day and the cry of many human hearts. It is likely that as many as 80% or more of all adults in our culture carry wounds from father deprivation. That includes most of us! So…Who is your Daddy really?

Table Of Contents

PREFACE xvii

Introduction xxi

Chapter One
Are Fathers Necessary? **23**

Chapter Two
War against Fathers **33**

Chapter Three
Defining Father Deprivation **43**

Chapter Four
The Parenting Process **55**

Chapter Five
Where Did All the Fathers Go? **73**

Chapter Six
Men and Father Deprivation **79**

Chapter Seven
Women and Father Deprivation **103**

Chapter Eight
Father Wounds and Homosexuality 117

Chapter Nine
Healing Father Wounds 121

Chapter Ten
The Steps for Healing 133

Chapter Eleven
Some Final Thoughts 147

Preface
"A Historical Perspective"

⸎⟶⸎

"The vanishing father is perhaps the central fact of the changing American family structure today. His virtual disappearance holds important consequences for his wife and his daughters, but I believe that the most critical impact is upon his sons. I also believe, I hope not too mystically, that the father-son relationship is at the core of any society in which the patterns of authority and creativeness are handed on chiefly through the males from generation to generation."

The Vanishing American Father

Max Lerner

This quote is from more than fifty years ago (McCall's Magazine, 1965). There have been some watchmen who have noticed and sounded warnings for a long time that the family in America is under attack. Dr. Paul Popenoe and his associates at the American Institute of Family Relations were writing and researching in the 1970's the changing role of the father and encouraging people to understand the father's importance.

Dr. Michael Lamb and his associates published one of the earlier text books (1976) compiling the research on the father's role in parenting and child development (The Role of the Father in Child Development). That volume stirred a great deal of attention from both theorists and researchers. The Third Edition was released in 1997. The research was very definitive as to the importance of the father, but the scientific and educational worlds were largely focused on the importance of the mother's role. While the scholarly world was beginning to wake up to the role of the father, the information was still buried in the halls of research.

Across America, even in the 70's, counselors and clinicians were seeing and dealing with the collateral damage of the deteriorating family. The clinical evidence was overwhelming as counselor's offices were overflowing with clients, mainly females, who were fighting to save their marriages and families. Over and over again women, who suffered from father deprivation, married men who suffered from father deprivation. The families were suffering from two wounded people trying to do something that they had not seen modeled in their own childhood. Dr. James Dobson signaled the pending crisis in 1980:

> *"The Western world stands at a great crossroads in its history. It is my opinion that our very survival as a people will depend upon the presence or absence of masculine leadership in millions of homes...I believe, with everything in me, that husbands hold the keys to the preservation of the family."*

The major cry was and still is about the vanishing father. But even with the warnings, America, in these fifty years, has moved into a "post-father" era. Society as a whole has lost the sense that fathers are important and that being a father is an honorable, important position to hold. The role of the father has become irrelevant in this culture.

Rumblings from the Grass Roots

In the early 90's there was a major move among men that was, to a large degree, a reaction to the strong feminist movement. A plethora of books and articles resulted.

Some men began to react to the negativity that was directed toward their gender. A new term, "gender shame" was created. It was used to define men who were ashamed of being men, who turned on their own gender because of all the "bad" credited to them.

Men began to band together and talk about their shame and insecurities. They began to share the grief they felt from not ever having known their fathers. Many men sought help through "Wildman" gatherings, men's conferences and drum beating rites of passage. These earlier vestiges began outside of the Christian community, but served as seed for the Promise Keeper movement that swept across the country.

Promise Keepers was a breath of fresh air for Christian men. Thousands of men gathered in stadiums across America and heard powerful presentations on manhood and how to become a better husband. They were challenged spiritually and healthy fathering was encouraged. Thousands of men found some personal healing and left the rallies with a determination to change their lives and to be different in their families.

Promise Keepers called men together and addressed the hunger that lay dormant in so many men in the church. Coach Bill McCartney, James Ryle and all of their leadership men struck a match that started blazes in many churches across America. Some of these sparks still smolder in different corners of the Christian world, but for the most part, the domesticated, feminized church smothered the flames and was never deeply impacted. The churches of America, if they believe there is a war going on against fathering, have never bought into the idea that this war is for the souls of men and boys in the American culture. So today, almost 50 years after Max Lerner made his statement, males make up only 35% of the average church attendance and fathers have become more and more irrelevant in the culture.

In the early 90's two key organizations were started: The National Fatherhood Initiative and The National Center for Fathering. Both of these organizations have contributed significantly to our understanding of the fatherlessness issue and the importance of the father in healthy personality development. Many research studies have been cataloged about the importance of fathering by psychologists like Michael Lamb and his associates and in hundreds of other settings. But, for the most part, governmental agencies and the judicial system function in ways that demonstrate they are either ignorant of the research or do not want to take the research into consideration. Churches still do not take action as pro-father resources and do little to attract and train men to be effective fathers. The National Center for Fathering offers training for men in churches, but they would be the first to tell you that they wish they could do more.

In June of 2008 the Global Fathering Initiative was established to address the issue of father deprivation around the globe and to mobilize the Church to become a pro-father resource. Global Fathering Initiative is based on the centrality of Father Love in the Christian gospel and the belief that the Church should be the advocate and voice for Father Love on the earth. GFI believes that the earthly father and his love for his family and children is a critical image of the Heavenly Father and His love that has been missing from many families around the globe. The goal of GFI is to challenge men to impact the world through fathering. It is to this end that this book has been written.

Introduction

I feared my father. I knew who my father was, but I didn't really know the man. Anger seemed to be the dominant emotion my father expressed with me. I felt I was a major disappointment to him. He died at age 56 when I was still a young man. We never connected in a loving meaningful way. I never felt his arms around me. I never heard him say *"I love you"* or *"I am proud of you."*

Today I know more about what was going on in my father's life. He was parenting the way he had been parented. My father had a tender giving heart. He was known as a generous man who would give the shirt off his back to someone in need. But he did not have the self-confidence to share his feelings with anyone except perhaps my mother.

Though I never heard my father say the actual words, I think he did love me and I think he was proud of me, at least I hope so. What a tragedy for both of us that we were never able to share those feelings. That same tragedy is repeated over and over again in our society.

When my counseling practice opened in 1972, I became aware of the pain of other adults who were raised with father deprivation. I saw the emotional wounds and the devastating effect on young men and women when they grew up without a loving, emotionally present, involved father.

I began to understand my life experiences better and started to see patterns in my life and in the lives of hundreds of adults with whom I had the privilege to work. I also began to investigate research conducted on the issue of father deprivation. This book is the outgrowth of over forty years of working and counseling with people who suffer from a lack of fathering.

Over the years and from more than 50,000 hours of counseling, I have concluded that as many as 80% of adults in contemporary U.S. society suffer to some degree from father deprivation. This book is about these wounded souls and it is dedicated to them. It is my prayer and my hope that this material, compiled from years of clinical work, will provide understanding and facilitate healing.

Waylon O. Ward

CHAPTER ONE

Are Fathers Necessary?

O ur culture is suffering from an epidemic of father deprivation. In fact, the whole world is. This is one of the most significant issues facing America, and it is a significant issue facing every nation on the globe. Christians and non-Christians alike suffer from father deprivation.

Father deprivation is what a child experiences when there is a lack of masculine parenting necessary for the child's personality to develop in a healthy manner. Father deprivation occurs when there is an absent or abusive father or when there is a non-involved male parent who is emotionally unavailable to the child. This is the experience of millions of children today and has been the experience of millions of people around the globe. People in every religion of the world suffer these wounds.

Many major crises facing our culture and the world today can be traced back to the fundamental loss of fathering and healthy masculinity in our society.

Impact of Lost Fathering

Here are some examples that demonstrate how the issue of father deprivation is a factor in cultural and world problems:

Wars and Terrorism: Most dictators or terrorist leaders (Hitler, Stalin, Marx, Castro, Chavez, Bin Laden, Ahmadinejad) come from homes where they experienced an abusive father, a father absent childhood or from a culture in which the lack of nurturing by fathers is the cultural norm.

Greed and Rogue Capitalism: More people who are determined to make the big score financially are seeking money and power to compensate for their lack of masculine competence. Getting rich is more important than feeding the hungry, caring for the environment or helping the homeless.

Leadership Vacuum: Organizations and institutions from governments and educational institutions to churches and homes are suffering from a deficit of ethical and competent leadership as more and more men abdicate their leadership roles.

AIDS: Rampant promiscuity among young males seeking to prove their sexual prowess and young girls seeking male attention feeds the increasing spread of AIDS and other sexually transmitted diseases.

Crime: The greatest predictor of crime in any given neighborhood is the number of father absent single parent families.

Gangs: Gangs in every country of the world are made up predominately of kids from fatherless homes.

Orphans: There are over 500 million orphans around the world who have no source for fathering or the protection and provision fathers provide.

Prison Populations: The increasing prison populations in the US and around the world are mainly fatherless or father deprived males. Fatherless sons are 300% more likely to be incarcerated in juvenile institutions than are sons raised with a father in the home.

Adolescent Murderers: The number of children and adolescents who commit murder is increasing and most of these grew up in fatherless homes.

Drugs and Addictions: Addictions are about medicating or covering pain. This includes the pain of fatherlessness and the pain caused by choices individuals make to medicate or cover this pain.

Sex Trade: Women are treated like objects and used for male gratification. The men who engage in these trades have little compassion and are unmoved by the pain they cause. This lack of feeling, empathy and compassion has been linked to being raised in fatherless environments.

"Single Mom" Families: The number of "Single Mom" families is on the increase across our culture. Among Black families, 71% of children are born out of wedlock and 80% of African-American children can expect to live a significant part of their childhood years apart from their fathers. 40% of all children in the US slept in a home last night where their biological father did not live.

Increase in Sex Crimes against Children: More and more children are suffering from sex crimes. The research shows that children raised without a father in the home are picked as targets more frequently than children living with a father in the home.

Religious Cults: Individuals raised without involved fathers, hungry for authority and structure from a father figure, fill the ranks of these groups.

Decline in the Christian Church: The Church has lost the message of Father Love and has not built strong male followers who have experienced Father Love. Many men have abandoned the church as being irrelevant for their daily struggles. In most nations of the world women make up 60 to 75% of church congregations.

Loss of Respect for Authority and Cultural Values: Many children raised in fatherless homes have not been raised with the boundaries that train children about politeness, hospitality and kindness. Disrespect for authority, abuse of freedoms and mistreatment of the elderly can all be traced to fatherlessness related issues.

Father deprivation is a critical issue around the globe and a major factor in the challenges facing our world.

The Critical Importance of Fathering

In The Search for Lost Fathering, James Schaller reminds his readers of the impressionable nature of the young child's heart and soul:

> *"A child's father is typically the first male to write his thoughts and feelings on his child's heart. Fathers, therefore, need to be sensitive to the messages their every word and action inscribe on that tender surface. Their children enter the world like tiny sponges, ready to absorb every little impression about themselves and their identity. They are unsure of who they are: Am I special? they ask. Am I valuable? Am I good? Am I merely an annoyance? Their fathers play a primary role in answering those questions."*

Schaller adds:

> *"It is not merely a child's identity that a father influences, but also his or her life goals, motivations, sexuality and relationships with other people."*

26

Yet we live in a society that has made fathers irrelevant. America, in the past fifty years, has moved into a "post-father" era. Society as a whole has lost the sense that fathers are important and that being a father is an honorable, important position to hold.

However, children know that fathering is important.

There was a nationally syndicated cartoon several years ago. It pictured a mother in a run down house with bullet holes in the window from a drive-by shooting. A young girl was pictured asking her mother: *"Mommy, where do Daddies come from?"*

A friend was appearing on a radio talk show. He and the host were talking about fathering and its importance with people who called in on the phone. A young male, probably eight or nine, called in and asked, *"Where can I buy a father?"*

I was counseling with a young divorced mother several years ago. She had two little girls about three and five years of age. The girls always sat in the waiting room while the mother worked on her issues in the counseling session. One day the mother said the girls asked if they could have a "session" with me. I agreed and two beautiful little girls came in looking very shy, but excited. They had a question for me: *"Would I be their Daddy?"*

What the Research Shows

In the last thirty years or so, sociology and psychology have begun to do research on fathering and the impact it has on the well-being and health of children. The National Fatherhood Initiative, the National Center for Fathering and the Global Fathering Initiative have been collecting research studies and teaching thousands of adults the importance of fathering. The statistics are overwhelming:

More than 40% of children sleep in homes every night where their biological father does not live.

80% of African-American children can expect to spend a significant part of their childhood apart from their fathers.

The likelihood that a young male will engage in criminal activity doubles if he is raised without a father.

72% of adolescents charged with murder grew up without their fathers.

60% of rapists, 70% of long term prison inmates, and 80 % of gang members are raised in fatherless homes.

80 to 90% of men in prison were raised without fathers.

We live in a post-father world. It is not a pretty situation anyway you look at it. But it can be different!

The research shows that regardless of race or economic status, children with involved, loving fathers are significantly more likely to do well in school, have a healthy self-esteem, exhibit empathy and pro-social behavior, and avoid high-risk behaviors such as drug use, truancy, and criminal activity compared to children who have uninvolved fathers (Father Facts).

This is the uncomfortable truth our society must face. However, people in general and the authorities in our society, for whatever reason, keep on degrading the role of the father.

The "Doofus" Dad

Anyone watching TV sees fathers presented as unnecessary or the dumb guy that mothers and teens "put up with." These degrading ads, plus the way fathers are portrayed in sitcoms, if they are included at all, have undermined even further the role and position of fathering. What healthy male would honestly seek to be like the portraits presented repeatedly on the movie screens and TV shows around the world?

Here is a quote from a FATHER FACTS essay entitled "Media & the State of Fatherhood" written by Jamin Warren.

"John Tierney of the New York Times heralded the arrival of 'the Doofus Dad'. 'Where did we fathers go wrong?' he writes in his Father's Day piece in 2005. 'We spend twice as much time with our kids as we did two decades ago, but on television we're oblivious (Jimmy Neutron), troubled (The Sopranos), deranged (Malcolm in the Middle) and generally incompetent (Everybody Loves Raymond). Paul Brownfield,

*of the LA Times, came to a similar conclusion the year before:
'He is being recycled, network season after network season,
as a hapless, benign man-child, tolerated (if he hasn't been
abandoned) by the wife and the butt of one-liners from child
actors who tell jokes as if they've spent July and August at
some kind of Friars Club summer camp.'"*

Even the benign Homer Simpson and Al Bundy, who replaced
Father Knows Best and Ward Cleaver of the 1950's, seem more
acceptable than current TV Dads. Perhaps the way some movies
leave fathers out all together is a kind gesture compared to the
degrading images so often portrayed.

Is it any wonder that men don't value fathering as an important
role for them to fulfill?

Without Value

A major issue affecting fathering in our culture is that many
males do not see that fathering has any value. Pressures from society
have caused many men to devalue their role in the family. They have
lost confidence that they are important to their children.

In child custody cases, the norm is still to grant the mother
custody unless she does not want it. Men who are loving caretakers
of the kids still have to fight for the right to have custody.

The evidence is obvious. The role of being a father has become
unimportant in our society. Courts, hospitals, schools, women and
even many men see Daddy as a less than admirable title. They don't
believe that these men have the power to affect their children, to
coach them to guide them. They don't believe that fatherhood is a
central purpose in men's lives.

When earthly fathers become irrelevant, then the Father Love of
God fades from awareness in the lives of most people. Down through
history, fathers have defined the important issues for children. What
was important, what is important to the fathers, becomes important
to their children. The only qualifier to this is when the truth is forced
or pushed on the children in a harsh judgmental way apart from a

sincere loving, emotional connected relationship. Otherwise, children absorb the values, faith and priorities of a loving father.

The church in general has become too much like the culture, picking up its values, reflecting its priorities instead of being light and salt. Church leadership has shifted from strong authentically masculine "spiritual fathers" to leadership made up of strong women and soft males. The feminized church has emphasized external image to attract the attention of the masses much like a woman dresses and presents herself to attract male attention. Fearful of not being significant, both the church and the woman settle for superficial "being noticed" versus serious deeper connections and quality of the relationship. Like the woman who thinks, *"If I can just catch a man's eye, then I can win him over,"* the church has developed image management for evangelism while ignoring the deeper issues of Father Love and the quality of relationships.

Is the role of the father a function that is no longer necessary in our culture? Can mothers raise healthy children without a male presence in a parenting role? Can Gay or Lesbian couples be good parents? There are many voices today saying that Dads are obsolete, except for financial support. Many men see providing financially as their major contribution to the family. But as two career families grow and wives sometimes earn as much or more money than their husbands, a father can be relegated to the secondary role even as a provider.

Because society, as a whole, has made fathers look ridiculous and unimportant, men have been stripped of their manhood. And children are the losers.

The context in which a child is raised determines how they respond to inputs they receive from the media and other resources. More from "Media & the State of Fatherhood":

"The chief problem with 'doofus dads' is context. Currently, there are more than 24 million children living without a father in the home. As many of these children are subjected to different images of fatherhood, they will have to make a key decision as to the type of father they would like to become. However, without an involved, responsible and committed

*father in their lives, they will have no image with which to
compare their own conceptions. I never thought that Homer
Simpson was a good dad, because I knew that my father
would never choke me every day, abandon my mother at a
marriage retreat to go fishing, or gain 70 lbs. to qualify for
worker's compensation. My father was always supportive
and fulfilled every obligation to be a good dad and would
never dream of emulating Homer's behaviors."*

It is time for men in America to wake up and understand how
important fathering is. Fathering is the most significant activity a
man can give his energy and resources to.

David Blankenhorn wrote in <u>Fatherless America</u>:

*"Fatherhood is a social role that obligates men to their
biological offspring. For two reasons, it is society's most
important role for men. First, fatherhood, more than any
other male activity, helps men to become good men: more
likely to obey the law, to be good citizens, and to think about
the needs of others. Put more abstractly, fatherhood bends
maleness—-in particular, male aggression—-toward pro-
social purposes. Second, fatherhood privileges children.
In this respect, fatherhood is a social invention designed to
supplement maternal investment in children with parental
investment in children."*

During an interview for a documentary-in-progress, Dr. Kyle
Pruett, a fatherhood expert with the Yale Child Study Center,
commented about the urgency of equipping fathers:

*"If you want to reduce gang membership, teen pregnancy,
dropping out of school, abuse and neglect of children, and
substance abuse, you can do it by engaging fathers early
and often in the lives of their children. We know this from the
science, we know it makes sense—it's not easy, but it absolutely works. It works on these problems like aspirin on a
headache. And our failure to connect the dots here with what*

we know is a huge unfinished problem is irresponsible. Our children absolutely deserve for us to stop fooling around and fix this."

The reality is that fixing this problem is not just a man's job. Healthy parenting takes a male and female to raise healthy children in a two gender world. A man and a woman, functioning as peers, sharing authority and responsibilities, make the healthiest parenting environment. Women and mothers must wake up and take notice of what is happening to fathering in our culture. The children they love and fight so hard for are being destroyed right in front of their eyes. If fathers are not restored to the proper parenting role in the family, children will continue to be deprived of the living environment that is most conducive to their well-being and happiness in later life. Our culture will continue to implode.

It is time for men to step up. Men, particularly we Christian men, should be angry as hell at all of these factors that are robbing us of our sons and daughters. Our most noble role as father has been attacked for too long. We must take the first step by engaging our hearts in the battle. It is time to take back the noble role of healthy fathering. If not now, when? If not you, who? How will you remember this day?

CHAPTER TWO

War against Fathers

There is a battle being fought daily for the family in every country, every city and on every farm in the world. The family is a major battle ground and children are the collateral damage over and over again. Father deprivation is the desolation that children are suffering as this battle rages.

The back drop necessary to enable you to understand the Father Deprivation epidemic in America and around the world is the spiritual nature and purpose of fathering. Fathering is more than biological; it is relational and spiritual. If you understand the designed purpose for fathering, then you can understand why spiritual warfare is focused on the father and the family.

Fatherhood is at the center of the universe and the relationship of the Heavenly Father and Son is the most central of all relationships. Leanne Payne, in her autobiography, <u>Heaven's Calling</u>, wrote: *"Fatherhood is smack at the core of the cosmos...and we impoverished moderns have largely lost this vital understanding."*

This spiritual nature and purpose of fathering is understood through the lens of Scripture and against the backdrop of the story about a great Father's love. The Biblical story, from first to last, is the story of a Father who has a great love for His Son. And this Father desired a large family, a people who would choose to lovingly adore and delight in His first born Son as much as He does (Luke 3:22, Matthew 17:2; John 17:26).

The atmosphere of Heaven is Father Love...God the Father's love for His Son and His love for those who love His Son. Worship is the love response of those the Father loves. When we pray "On earth as it is in Heaven" we are praying for the Father's love to be experienced on earth as it is in Heaven. The Kingdom of God is about Fathering and Fathering is the way the Kingdom works on earth.

The Father's Love

The story of a Father loving a Son and building a family to love and honor His Son is the storyline of the Scriptures and the summation of the Gospel story. Christianity is based on a loving Father who gave His Son so that all mankind could experience the love of the Father (John 3:16) and choose to love the Son in return. The Cross and the Atonement are what God did to make it possible for us to call Him "Abba, Father". The Son came into the world to reveal the nature of His Father's heart (John 12:45, 14:9). He became "the Lamb of God who takes away the sin of the world" (John 1:29). The Cross that Jesus died on is the open door into God's heart for all mankind who will enter in (Romans 5:8). The Kingdom of God includes all the members of the Father's family who have entered in and love and honor the Son as the Father does.

> *"The supernatural interventions of God were done to reveal the extravagant heart of the Father for people. Every miracle is a revelation of His nature. And in that revelation is embedded an invitation for relationship."*
> Bill Johnson, <u>When Heaven Invades Earth</u>

God's loving heart is open because of the Cross; God's Spirit is actively inviting all mankind into relationship with Him.

The Family of God

The story in the Christian message is this story of the Father wooing the hearts of mankind through His love and bringing men and women into His spiritual family through the Cross of His Son. Love, grace and forgiveness are the heart of the Father for all His children; they are the heart of true Christianity. The heart of God is open to all because of what Jesus did, but not all mankind will respond and enter into this relationship with the Father.

The true Church is made up of those who respond to the open heart of the Father. These are the members of the family created by the Father who called many sons and daughters (Romans 8:29). It is made up of the sons and daughters...the children of the Father... who are to *"make known the manifold wisdom of God to the rulers and authorities in the heavenly realm"* (Ephesians 3: 10-11) *"... according to His eternal purpose which He accomplished in Christ Jesus our Lord."*

In His prayer in John 17, Jesus made two enlightening statements about the Father's love. First, in verse 23 He stated that God the Father loves "them" (those who believe in Christ) as much as He, the Father, loved the Son. God the Father loves all of those who have been spiritually born into His family as much as He loves his only begotten Son.

The second statement Jesus makes is in John 17:26. He prays that the love the Father has for Him (Jesus) may be in all of those who have been born into His family. Jesus prays that the Father's love for Him would be in the heart of every member of the family. God wants all of His family members to love the Son as much as He does. This family is the true Church. It is the authority on the Father's Love because this love is the root of the gospel message and the life blood of the Church.

Spiritual Warfare

Spiritual warfare on the earth is conducted by Satan to create a planet deprived of the Father's love. One critical component the enemy uses is to structure an environment that removes men from the family, creating earthly father deprivation. Since the earthly father is designed to be a picture of the Heavenly Father, the enemy hates fathering with a passion. And Satan desires to erase any image or reflection of the Heavenly Father off the globe.

Some Christian authorities believe Satan attacks fathering so vehemently because he himself cannot procreate and he is angry at humans who can. Satan cannot reproduce himself through procreation, and his envy and jealousy at humans who can has burned furiously throughout the centuries. Families, mothers and fathers are all attacked by him in his all-out war to destroy Father Love on the earth.

Wherever and whenever Satan has influenced humans, he has always worked to get human parents to sacrifice their children, whether it is to some idol in the ancient world or to a career or personal ego pursuits in this modern age. By making the human father irrelevant, the enemy is striking at the Heavenly Father, seeking to undermine His influence in the world by destroying those who portray the heavenly Father's character and attributes to their offspring.

But the Good News is that our Father in Heaven has defeated Satan through the Cross of Jesus!

A Pro-Father Faith

The Christian faith is at its very core pro-father. In the Old Testament, Abraham, Moses, David and some of the Prophets recognized God as "Father" and Israel was seen as the child or son of God, but the God presented in the Scriptures was not fully known as a "loving personal Father" until Jesus came and revealed Him as such. In fact, few if any religions throughout history have ever in any way pictured God as a "loving personal Father."

In the Old Testament, the Jewish nation had an image of God who was the "father and loving caregiver" of all creation (Deuteronomy 32:6, Isaiah 64:8, Malachi 2:10) and Israel in particular, but the image of God was not one of a God who is a personal loving father.

Today, the concept of a God who is a loving Father is unknown in the world except within Christianity. None of the world's religions teach about a personal loving God who is like a father. An example of this is seen in Islam. The perspective within Islam is pictured in the quotes within the Mosque of Omar in Jerusalem. *"Allah is not a father. He has no sons."* is written over a door and on one wall there is another inscription about Jesus being a prophet. In this inscription is included the statement: *"It is not for Allah to take a son."*

Jesus from His childhood (Luke 2:49), in the beginning of His ministry (Matthew 5-6) and until his Ascension (Acts 1), called God His Father and He taught His followers to do the same. Jesus brought the transcendent God of the Old Testament world into the immanent present experience as a loving Father. He said He was an incarnation of this loving Father so that those who had seen Him had seen the Father (John 12:45; 14:9).

The Christian faith teaches that all believers are to be transformed so that their internal nature and character are Christ-like. When their internal nature becomes Christ-like, then their external behaviors can become Christ-like (Ephesians 4:12-13; Romans 12:2; II Corinthians 3:18; Galatians 5:22-23). Christian parents are to be a living incarnation of the character and nature of God so their children's hearts will be prepared to encounter Christ on their own. Mothers and fathers, individually and in their relationships, are to both represent and model the character and nature of God for their children.

> *"The Church is to be the manifestation of the Father's heart to the world. We are carriers of His presence, doers of His will; the Father's business flows from His heart . . . His presence always reveals His heart."*
>
> Bill Johnson, <u>When Heaven Invades Earth</u>

Earthly fathering is the idea of the Creator; "Father" is the name His Son taught His creatures to use when we pray. Earthly fathering is to present a picture for all children of the loving heart of the Heavenly Father.

Earthly Fathers

Earthly fathers are to be a picture of the Heavenly Father's love. Children, as they grow up, should have an experience with a loving adoring father who accepts them and delights in them, a father who desires the best for them and encourages them to become all that they can be. This human father is to prepare the hearts of his children to be open to the love of God and a relationship with the Heavenly Father. Earthly fathers are intended to be incarnations of the nature of the Father and models of how the Heavenly Father loves His children, preparing the children to receive the love that God offers to them.

A Father's Love is at the Heart of the Christian Faith. Restoring Father Love to the center of the Church's mission to the world should be a priority. Human fathers are meant to be pictures of the Heavenly Father's love and, if they drop the ball, than the next generation loses out. The lack of this emphasis is a major factor in the church's failure to successfully accomplish intergenerational transfer of the faith to younger generations.

Soul Construction

Fathering is one of the most important relationships any man can engage in because it is critical to constructing the souls of his children. Parenting, including both fathers and mothers, is important because it is the God-ordained means for growing a human soul and constructing the human personality. No person should ever take casually the soul of another, particularly the souls of his children. Fathers are an integral part of soul construction in their children's lives. It is not a matter of whether or not you imprint and shape your child's soul, it is a matter of whether you imprint that soul to be receptive of a loving Heavenly Father or if you imprint that child's soul to fear or distrust the idea of a Father God.

The soul is the internal person, the person we cannot see. We experience a person's soul when we interact with his personality. The individual's personality is the external expression of their soul, and parents are engaged in the critical activity of soul construction with their children. There's a great old saying: *"Children are like wet cement. Everything that touches their lives leaves an imprint."* Parents imprint the souls of their children.

Fathering is important because the human soul needs both gender parents to grow and mature as God intended. Fathers can only fulfill their Divine assignment as men in a right relationship with God. The realization of the great responsibility a father has in helping structure a child's soul for the glory of God should drive every man to his knees. Each man is inadequate in his human abilities. We all need the indwelling power of God for the awesome job of being a father.

A Supernatural Response

The healing and restoring of men, women and families is a priority in the heart of God. He is healing and restoring men to be healthy loving fathers. This book is about the supernatural activity of God to restore Father Love on earth. We have prayed *"On earth as it is in Heaven"* (Matthew 6:10); Father Love is the atmosphere of heaven. To bring Heaven to earth, to restore the relationships between fathers and their children, requires an intervention of the Holy Spirit. Restored relationships...hearts healed, forgiveness given and received...are all products of Kingdom power expressed on earth.

When Heaven invades earth, it is an expression of the Father's heart, an outpouring of God's love on humanity. Earthly fathers were designed to be flesh and blood realities on earth of the love of this unseen God.

The healing and restoring of broken hearts and broken relationships is accomplished by the Holy Spirit using the Word of God (both spoken and written) and the people of God. Healing father wounds is the work of the Holy Spirit just as surely as raising the dead and healing the sick are works of the Spirit.

I believe God is just as interested in healing broken relationships and restoring families as He is in healing the sick and enabling the lame to walk (Isaiah 61). Kingdom living is about Kingdom relationships, and the atmosphere of Heaven is likely to show up when we are living out Jesus' great relational mandate: *"Love one another as I have loved you"* (John 13:34-35). Jesus told His followers to love one another as He has loved them and, for parents, this includes loving your children the way Jesus has loved you. Healing the wounds from father deprivation, absence and abuse requires spiritual and emotional healing.

This book is about the miraculous healings that God wants to accomplish (Malachi 4:6; Luke 1:17). Healing the father wound is a component of what God wants to do on the earth; it is one of the keys *"to make ready a people prepared for the Lord."*

Many pastors, leaders and teachers are waiting for an outpouring of Father Love from the Heavenly Father on earth as a critical component of the last great revival that will sweep the globe. But are we now in those end times? Some believe we are. However, regardless of your beliefs about a great end time harvest, I believe that God is wanting to do a major work now to turn the hearts of fathers to their children and the hearts of children to their fathers. It is time now, as God pours out His Spirit on our world, that we work to help men be transformed into healthy fathers who picture the Heavenly Father on this earth. It is time now for broken hearts to be healed, relationships to be restored and the noble role of the earthly father to flourish on the earth.

A Passionate Desire

God put a passionate desire in my heart many years ago, a desire to see earthly fathers restored to their noble role, picturing God the Father to their children. For years, when I have spoken on the subject of father deprivation, I have made this statement: *"If God would grant me one wish, one miracle, I would put healthy fathers back in the homes."* The only way this can happen is through a powerful move of God's Spirit.

All healing is from God, either by His design or by His intervention. He created our bodies to have powerful self-healing properties, but there are times His direct intervention is needed. It is the same within individuals, families and cultures. To see the transformation of a person's soul, to experience the healing of a relationship, to see the healing in a family, to see a culture healed, these are miraculous touches from God.

I have observed the miraculous in the counseling room for forty years:

Lives, chained by pain, set free.

Broken hearts healed.

Broken spirits restored.

Broken relationships made whole.

Father wounds healed.

These individuals all needed a touch of the healing that only the Spirit of God can give. Many of these suffered from father wounds. I know God is in the healing business and that He can heal father wounds. I have seen it happen; I have experienced that healing in my own life.

This passion has possessed me. The Spirit of God has taught me and empowered me. As long as the Father enables me, I will spend the rest of my life challenging men to be what God intended them to be, because only Jesus can make healthy Godly men and fathers who picture accurately the nature and character of God to their wives and children.

If we pray and teach accurately the love of the Father revealed through Jesus, if we can enable thousands of men and women to find healing for their childhood father wounds, if we can train thousands of men to be healthy fathers, and if men and women can join together and establish a pro-father agenda in the churches of America, then we can see God begin to bring a mighty move of His Spirit around the globe. If we undertake this mission without the empowering of the Holy Spirit, than we might as well take a tea cup and try to empty the oceans. I believe that God is moving in the area of healing father wounds and restoring the hearts of fathers to their children and the hearts of the children to their fathers. I believe that He is looking for men and women who will join Him in this great move of His Spirit.

A key aspect of the Kingdom of God is Fathering and all of us in this Kingdom are to be Fathered by God and to engage in Fathering.

"O Loving Father, my Abba. We ask that You bring healing to the people who suffer from wounds of a father. We ask that You establish the noble role of fathering on the earth again. We ask that You put healthy fathers back in homes all over the globe so that mothers and children have an accurate picture of Your Father love. Our prayer is that Father Love will fill the earth and become the reality of the Kingdom on earth. The Harvest is ready, please raise up men to be fathers to a fatherless world. As it is in Heaven, let it be here on earth. This is our prayer. Amen."

CHAPTER THREE

Defining Father Deprivation

Healthy fathering must begin with healthy authentic masculinity. The two are vitally connected; you do not get one without the other. Perfection is not the qualifying characteristic, but persistent, intentional pursuit is the key. Men must understand that true masculinity is something that is high and noble, not simply tough and isolating. Men learn from other men how to become healthy masculine males. True masculinity is caught from other men; men grow and change in gender specific relationships.

Father deprivation is better understood when seen against the backdrop of healthy authentic masculinity. What does healthy authentic masculinity look like?

LeAnne Payne, in her excellent book <u>Crisis in Masculinity</u> gives a brief defining statement:

> *"The power to honor the truth, to speak it and be it, is at the heart of true masculinity."*

Based on that foundation, here is a list of characteristics that a healthy authentically masculine man will agree with and work to attain. Again, remember that perfection is not the qualifying characteristic, but persistent, intentional pursuit is the key.

1. His highest priority is his relationship with God, his Heavenly Father.
2. His public and private life are lived in a congruent and authentic way.
3. He is learning to experience, feel and express his true feelings.
4. His relationships with other men are loving, transparent and caring.
5. Except for God the Father, his wife has priority over all other relationships in his life.
6. All individuals of the opposite sex are viewed and treated with honor and respect.
7. He expresses anger appropriately.
8. Perseverance is his attitude under stress and trial.
9. All of his relationships are characterized by maturity, strength and gentleness.
10. The mantle of leadership is understood and accepted in his family, friendships and business world.
11. His family has a high priority. He does everything in his power to provide for and protect them.
12. Finances are managed with planning and integrity; he includes his wife in important financial decisions.
13. Addictions are not an issue in his life.

These characteristics are produced by the Spirit of God working in the heart and soul of men. As the Spirit works in the man's soul, the man takes on a strong family likeness to Jesus.

"And we all, who with unveiled faces contemplate the Lord's glory, are being transformed into His image with ever increasing glory, which comes from the Lord who is the Spirit."
II Corinthians 3:18

With this understanding of healthy authentic masculinity, the idea of healthy fathering is much easier to understand. The dysfunctional aspects of neglectful father deprivation stick out like a sore thumb. Dysfunctional fathering is the outworking of unhealthy masculinity trying to parent children.

Usually these unhealthy behaviors are unintentional and unplanned, the results of unhealthy issues in a man's life, often from the man's own childhood. Few fathers start out intending to mistreat their children, but healthy fathering has to be an intentional planned effort for all men. Unconscious unhealthy issues in a man get expressed when the stress of daily life kicks in. The more healthy and authentic a man is, the better father he will be.

Unhealthy dysfunctional fathering robs children of the God-ordained emotional and relational interaction needed for the development of a healthy soul and personality. We can divide unhealthy fathering into three categories: Father Absence, Father Abuse, and Father Deprivation. Since a child who experiences father absence or father abuse also experiences father deprivation, we have used Father Deprivation as a specific category and also as an overall inclusive description of all the wounds children experience. When a child experiences either father absence or father abuse, he also experiences the emotional wounding that every father-deprived child experiences.

Father Deprivation

Father-Deprivation is what a child experiences when there is a lack of masculine parenting necessary for the child's personality to develop in a healthy manner. Father Deprivation occurs when there is a non-involved male parent who is not emotionally available to, or not involved with, the child. Father Deprivation happens in church-going Christian families as well as in non-Christian families.

For a child to experience appropriate masculine parenting, the male parent must make emotional contact with the child on a regular basis; the father must be emotionally invested in the life of the child. This means that father and child have regular eye to eye contact, meaningful interactions and warm loving hugs and physical affection shared on a regular basis. Without these, children suffer emotional soul wounds and their personalities are marked by certain emotional vulnerabilities.

Father-deprived children are sometimes raised in families where there is a male parent figure physically present, but not emotionally connected. The child suffers chronic emotional neglect from the male parent. These non-involved, non-emotional, non-relational fathers do not have a warm, affectionate, loving, attentive, quality relationship with their children. The father's lack of availability may be due to addiction, abuse, repression, or simply an inability to experience his own emotions or feelings.

In the popular book, <u>Iron John</u>, written by Robert Bly, the author concluded:

> *"Not seeing your father when you are small, having a remote father, an absent father, a workaholic father, is an injury... perhaps the most damaging of all."*

For millions of children today this is their experience. This is the age of the "Vanishing Father". Tonight in America, approximately 40% of children will sleep in a home where their biological father does not live. Untold thousands of others will sleep in a house with a father they feel does not care about them.

An almost infinite variety of patterns of father deprivation can exist and a number of other factors may increase the effects and wounds due to the lack of healthy fathering. Michael Lamb in his book <u>The Role of the Father in Child Development</u>, lists a number of the factors that are involved:

> *"...length of separation from the father, type of separation (constant, intermittent, temporary, etc.); cause of separation (divorce, death of father, etc.); the child's age, sex, and constitutional characteristics; the mother's reaction to husband absence; the quality of mother-child interaction; the family's socioeconomic status; and the availability of surrogate models . . ."*

As Lamb indicates, the presence of other adult male figures in a child's life can have a dramatic lessening of the fatherless effect:

"Father absent children may not be paternally deprived if they have adequate father surrogates, or they may be less paternally deprived than are many father present children."

To the degree the father is uninvolved and to the degree the child has no effective male influence to help compensate, to that degree the child will be impacted. The presence of any male figure (step-father, grandfather, uncle, older brother, teacher, coach, friend's Dad, etc. - all sources of masculine parenting) who is emotionally involved with the child, helps alleviate the effects of father deprivation. Surrogate fathering can be very effective.

Father Abuse

Father Abuse is a critical problem around the world. Unfortunately, even in Christian homes, emotionally wounded and unhealed adult Christians have abused their children physically, emotionally and sexually. Being 'born-again" does not insure emotional healing; wounded parents often wound their children.

However, statistics show that children living with both biological parents are far less likely to be abused than children living in other arrangements. Serious abuse and neglect are lowest in households with married biological parents and highest in homes in which the mother lives with a partner who is not the biological parent of her children. The vast majority of child physical and sexual abuse is committed in single-parent homes, homes usually where the father is not present. The father, more than a step-father or live-in male, is the parent likely to be the protector of children. The presence of a father places the child at lesser risk for child sexual abuse and a British study found children are up to 33 times more likely to be abused when a live-in boyfriend or stepfather is present than in an intact family.

Father abuse can be physical abuse (hitting, slapping, etc.), verbal abuse (name calling, cursing, being judgmental or critical, screaming, etc.) and sexual abuse (inappropriate touching, fondling, sexual stimulation, incest, rape, etc.). These types of abuse can be from a biological father, a step-father, a surrogate father figure, a family member or a stranger, but the child is always the victim. The closer more trusting the relationship is, the greater the wounding and violation to the child's soul.

No father should ever abuse his child; fathers who do, leave wounds and scars that forever change a child's life. These children experience father deprivation of the worst kind. Dr. James Schaller says:

> *"A father who beats, molests, verbally degrades, disrupts the stability of the home by his alcohol, gambling, drugs, or moodiness is an anti-father. He sucks the life from the veins of his family; he functions as an emotional black hole. He steals the carefree laughter of childhood. Such a father produces a large amount of psychic orphanhood in his children, forcing them to function as emotional orphans, even though both parents are still alive."*

Children who have been hurt by a father and who resent their father's attitudes and behaviors often relate to others the same way the father related to them. Leonard Shergold, in his book <u>Soul Murder: The Effects of Childhood Abuse and Deprivation</u>, makes the case that abused children often do a reversal in their minds and conclude that the "bad" behavior of their parent is really "good" behavior so the child can have a sense that someone is emotionally on his side. Identification with the abuser is better than having no one, and these children often become adults who abuse their children.

Unfortunately there are some unhealthy, deeply wounded Christian men who are abusive.

Father Absence

Father-Absent children are children raised in families where there is no significant male parent figure available for a major portion of time. This absence may be due to death, divorce, work, career (military and/or other), prison or abandonment. These children do not receive adequate male parenting and carry deep emotional soul wounds; often their personalities are marked with emotional vulner-abilities. Again, the presence of any male figure, who serves as a source of masculine energy, helps alleviate the effects of father-depri-vation. Even the presence of other male peers (buddies, brothers, friends) can alleviate some of the effects of father absence. This is why healthy group relationships, spiritual fathers and surrogate fathers can be effective.

The National Fatherhood Initiative (www.fatherhood.org) has conducted extensive research on the issue of father absence and has developed many helpful initiatives to try to reverse this trend in our culture. The research data they have compiled demonstrates a painful reality for far too many American children. Most of the research data cited in this book comes from the book Father Facts, published by the National Fatherhood Initiative. The research is over-whelming; statistics do not lie and these numbers can be multiplied by thousands. Fatherlessness is an epidemic that is destroying the well-being of families, children and society. It is not just producing havoc in America, but all over the world.

Vulnerability to Sins

The Christian faith affirms the worth and value of every human being around the world from birth. Every person is created in the image of God and has great worth and value because of the image he/she bears. Each person is created as a God-shaped vessel intended to be filled by the Spirit of God. And this God-shaped image gives all men and women value and worth.

When God created mankind and the earth, the Scriptures describe it as "good". Adam and Eve were created in the image of God and walked with Him in the Garden. They were in perfect communion with God and with each other. They were in a right relationship with their Father, walking and talking with Him. God gave them authority over the Garden and certain assignments to fulfill (Genesis 1:27-28).

When Adam and Eve disobeyed the one rule that God had given them and ate the forbidden fruit, they unwittingly gave their authority over the world into Satan's control. Theologians called this event the Fall (Genesis 3). After the Fall, the communion between God and Adam and Eve was broken as was their communion with each other. Sin entered the world, and all mankind would be born separated from God from that point forward.

All men and women born into this fallen world have a nature that is bent toward self and the created world instead of being unbent and connected with God. All mankind are created by God, but are born disconnected spiritually from God as empty vessels. This "bent condition", as C. S. Lewis termed it, is the nature of all human beings. Every person has this nature that chooses self-centeredness over and against God-centeredness. Theologians call this the "sin nature".

Since every person has this sin nature, the question is why does one person choose one type of sin and another person chooses another type of sin? Since all mankind are sinners from birth, why does one person choose to be a murderer, another chooses to be a heterosexual sinner, another chooses homosexual sin and still another chooses to be a thief? (See I Corinthians 6:9-10.)

The type of sin people choose has to do with the vulnerabilities they carry from their family of origin. The wounds they experience in childhood cause them to be vulnerable to one form of sinful behavior as opposed to another. The wounds children experience set the stage for their lifestyle as they choose different behaviors to try to fill the emptiness, compensate for their vulnerabilities and heal their wounds.

The wounds of father deprivation, father absence and father abuse all create vulnerabilities in children's lives and, to a large degree, determine the types of sin they choose. The beginning for all of their healings is coming to a loving Heavenly Father through the Cross of Jesus. This is the only way to heal our "Orphan Hearts".

The Orphan Heart

People who suffer father wounds, whether it is from father abuse, father absence or father deprivation, develop thoughts and feelings that can be identified as coming from an "orphan's heart". They develop behavioral patterns, attitudes, thoughts and feelings similar to what orphans experience. The original orphans were Adam and Eve after the Fall, and all humans have been born separated from God since that moment in history. Thus the roots of the orphan heart lie in the basic sin nature of man dating back to the Fall. Parents, who are sinners, pass on to their children the sinful consequences of their own orphan hearts.

The orphan heart is characterized by shame, guilt, fear and anger. The lies of Satan create orphan thinking and the individual feels he has no safe place, no home. Time and time again people in counseling have tearfully poured out the pain and fears of not being wanted, not being important. Many of the issues they bring into counseling are really their ways of trying to hide or bury the pain of an orphan heart behind counterfeit comforts.

A person with an orphan heart will often be independent, self-reliant, hostile, and contentious, with no sense of home, belonging or of being a loved child. Here are some of the attitudes and behaviors that people with an orphan heart can often demonstrate:

- They feel disconnected, on the outside looking in.
- They feel unappreciated and feel that no one appreciates what they do.
- They look for the high place, the place where they are recognized and affirmed...special.
- They expect rejection, hurt, and fear abandonment.
- They are covetous and envy the success and blessings of others.
- They are overly concerned about their rights being violated.

- They take offense easily.
- They don't feel the pain they cause others.
- They distrust authority. They run and hide, feeling unworthy.
- They accept the crumbs because they don't feel worthy of the banquet.
- Since they have experienced rejection and abandonment, they carry the expectation of being rejected and abandoned by God.
- They think that God does good things for others and wonder why He won't do the same for them.
- They feel they have to strive, out-perform and out-do everybody else to succeed, yet nobody notices or even cares how hard they work.
- They are self absorbed and their lives are centered around their personal wants and desires.
- They believe that nothing is going to ever change; their lives are hard and always will be. It is hard for them to keep up their hope.
- They keep expecting that the other shoe will drop and the worst will happen.
- They abandon grace and substitute legalism as the way to be right before God. They are always looking for what they did wrong or for the secret verse that will tell them what they have to do to have God's favor.

The orphan's heart feels separation from God, separation from any sense of having a real safe place or home and separation from friends and family.

The orphan heart feels:

- There is no God who cares about me.
- There is no safe place for me to be.
- There is no one who really cares about me.
- I have no father, no home and no family.

The wounds of the father, contaminated by the lies of Satan, create the orphan heart. All of us, because of the Fall, experience some of these thoughts and feelings at certain times during our lives. When these thoughts and feelings dominate our lives, we are suffering from an orphan's heart. The cure for the orphan heart is understanding the Fatherhood of God and His love for each of us individually. We will discuss healing the father wound in later chapters of this book.

What the Research Shows

Children with a healthy father relationship do not have a strong sense of an orphan heart and have fewer vulnerabilities then those who suffer from some form of father deprivation, absence or abuse. Research conclusively shows that children with involved, loving fathers are significantly more likely to do well in school, have a healthier self-esteem, exhibit empathy and pro-social behavior, and avoid high-risk behaviors such as drug use, truancy, and criminal activity compared to children who have uninvolved fathers.

The research conducted over the past fifty years confirms that involved fathers make a huge difference in their children's lives. Yet the "Dad Difference" is almost totally ignored by politicians, law makers and the general population as a whole.

The writing is on the wall: America's not doing so well in a post-father era. It is time to wake up and smell the coffee. We need to bring Daddy back! Maybe we don't want the patriarchal, iron-fisted father or the sweet and wise Ward Cleaver version, but we do need a male parent figure in American homes.

Could we not encourage men to once again pick up the mantle of fatherhood? He does not have to be all-knowing, always right, "faster than a speeding bullet." Just being a loving, healthy masculine human being would be great for starters.

CHAPTER FOUR

The Parenting Process

There are two processes that God designed and ordained which every human being must participate in to reach maturity:

1) Parenting Process
2) Growth Process

These two processes are as hard wired into mankind as is gravity in the universe. Every new person coming into the world must experience these two processes to reach maturity. Even Jesus experienced these same two processes in His childhood (Luke 2:52).

Parenting Process

The human parenting process is unique among all of the animal kingdom. While there are similarities, the length of time that human parents are needed in parenting their offspring is much lengthier than any other animal's involvement with their offspring. All other animals have a brief parenting experience. Their young all reach mature adulthood in less than five years, while human offspring require eighteen years or longer.

Humans spend anywhere from one third to one half of their lives involved in either being parented or actively parenting their own children. Many couples, when they spread out their child bearing years (either by choice or by having a "surprise" pregnancy after most of the children are grown), can spend their whole lives being parented and being a parent.

The extended dependency and vulnerability of human offspring is related to complexities in the development of the human personality. The human personality is formed, deformed and transformed in relationships; the primary relationships are those within the family of origin.

There are two key components of the parenting process as God designed it. The first of these is the authoritative component and the second is the relational component.

The authoritative component was designed by God for the protection of the young child and to provide boundaries and structure for the child. As the child grows, he internalizes the structure and learns about boundaries so that he becomes able to govern his own life. As the child matures, the parents relax the authoritative component so that the child learns to rule his own life as he internalizes what he learned from his parents. If his parents have not exercised their authority in an appropriate manner and taught appropriate boundaries, then the child has difficulty in moving into healthy self-governing adulthood.

The relational component is the loving and nurturing component of the parenting process. The parents create an atmosphere of unconditional love and acceptance for the child and this is the atmosphere and context in which the authoritative component is exercised. Rules without relationship lead to rebellion, so the authoritative component is effective when the child knows he is loved and delighted in by both parents. Unlike the authoritative component, the relational component should never cease...it should grow stronger as the child matures into healthy adulthood.

Growth Process

To grow to physical maturity is a process that takes longer for different species, but most animals reach maturity within four or five years. Growth can be defined as positive change towards maturity; every living species, plant or animal, grows. To stop growing is to die, and this is true spiritually, mentally and physically. The immature are growing toward maturity, and this process is an absolute necessity for all living species. The human offspring has a longer period of vulnerability and requires many more years for the growth process than any other animal.

Most human beings have reached physical maturity by age 18; however, many authorities agree that human beings do not reach emotional maturity until age 30 or later. Experts believe that this lengthier growth and developmental process is due to the complexities and vulnerabilities of the human offspring and the ingredients required for the development of the human soul and personality.

Understanding the Family System

"The idea...that children of either sex can get along satisfactorily, in a two-sexed world, with the patterns furnished them by only one sex, is distinctly harmful. They need to have patterns of both sexes from infancy onward."

Paul Popenoe
American Institute of Family Relations

The growth process is not just biological; it is emotional and relational. The human soul and personality develop through interactions with parents, siblings, extended family members and peer relationships. The most fundamental of these relationships are those of the family of origin, particularly the relationships with the female parent and the male parent.

Parental involvement means that the parent is emotionally connected and interactive with the child at every stage of life. The relationships grow and change as the child grows, but both parents are significant and important from birth throughout the whole process and afterwards into the adult years.

Armand M. Nicholi, a Harvard psychiatrist, summarized his perspective on this point:

> *"If any factor influences the character development and emotional stability of an individual, it is the quality of the relationships he or she experiences as a child with both parents. Conversely, if people suffering from severe, non-organic emotional illness have one experience in common, it is the absence of a parent through death, divorce, a time-demanding job, or for other reasons."*

The Functional Family System
(The following material goes with the diagram on page 62.)

By God's design, parenting and growth were meant to take place in the context of our individual families of origin, the families that a child is born into. Since the world we live in is a fallen world and God's original design has been distorted, the family system and structure He designed has become almost unrecognizable in many situations. But this does not mean that His design is not foundational and observable in today's culture.

Looking at the family system as He intended it to be enables us to see a simplified developmental scheme that helps explain a complex process. This paradigm has been presented to thousands of individuals in counseling and in audiences for more than forty years. It is not intended to be a complete presentation of developmental psychology. While the diagram gives you a way of understanding parenting which promotes healthy development, it also enables you to understand how the family system has been distorted in our culture.

Remember that God designed the human soul and personality to be formed, deformed and transformed in relationships. We are who we are because of the relationships we experienced in our early years of life.

Every child goes through three stages in their relationships with their parents during development from infancy to adulthood. In all three stages, a balance of masculine and feminine parenting is necessary. In each stage one parent may dominate, but the presence of the other parent is critical for balance and the healthy development of the child.

While there are some similarities to other paradigms, there is one major difference. These other paradigms emphasized the sexual urge as the explanation for different stages of development. This paradigm emphasizes the God designed, natural relationships as the key issues in the child's development. Children are designed by God to have relational needs that are gender specific and which have nothing to do with sexual urges in the child's development. God intended for the human personality to grow and develop in the context of loving relationships.

Nurturing Stage:
Birth to Approximately Age Three

The young infant/child does not distinguish between masculine and feminine gender and parenting at this stage of development. He or she experiences both gender parents as nurturing. This is the stage when trust is being developed in the child. During this stage a child develops positive or negative expectations about life.

The parent's involvement, consistently meeting the physical and emotional needs of the child, builds confidence in the child that he can expect that his needs will be met. When he needs to eat, food will be provided. When he needs to have his diaper changed, someone will be there for him. When he is frightened, there will be a safe place for him. When he is tired, he will be able to sleep in a safe place. It is this consistent provision of the basic needs in life that distinguishes the life an orphan and a child who has a loving safe home. The orphan's life is permeated with fear; the child with a loving family experience develops an attitude of trust and positive expectancy toward the future.

God's intention was that both gender parents have a personal emotional and physical involvement with the child during these first three years of life and, if this does not happen, the child's ability to trust is greatly affected. There is some clinical data that indicates that when the father is absent, the child has more distrust toward males and when the mother is absent during this stage there is more distrust of females.

This early stage also sets the foundation for a child's future understanding of God and His loving nature. A child who has warm loving parents will have an expectation that God will be like his/her Mom and Dad.

Transition: Somewhere around three years of age.

The child, at approximately three years of age, discovers that his/her body is either like Mommy's or like Daddy's. This discovery marks the transition into the next stage.

Opposite Gender Parenting Stage:
Approximately Age Three to Ten

In this stage of development, the parent of the opposite sex has the most significant influence on the child's development, but parenting from the same sex parent is critical to maintain the balance in the developmental process and to prepare the child for the next transition. The primary emotional needs a child has during this stage are for affection and attention from the parent of the opposite sex.

Transition: Somewhere from eight until ten years of age.

As the early signs of puberty begin, the child shifts his or her gender focus from the parent of the opposite sex to the parent of the same sex. This usually happens between the ages of eight and ten, but it varies significantly with different children.

Same Gender Parenting Stage:
Approximately Age Ten to Adult

In this stage of development, the parent of the same gender has the most significant influence on the child's development, but parenting from the opposite gender parent is critical for balance in the process. The primary emotional needs a child has during this stage are for modeling and affirmation. The child is learning how to be an adult male or female, a process that continues into the young adult years.

The healthier the female parent is, the healthier the male parent is and the healthier their marital relationship is, then the healthier the children raised in that home will be. Parents are to function in a synergistic manner with the balance between the genders being maintained. This is a picture of how parenting was designed by God to function. In this fallen world, this design has become contaminated and distorted by the enemy of the human soul.

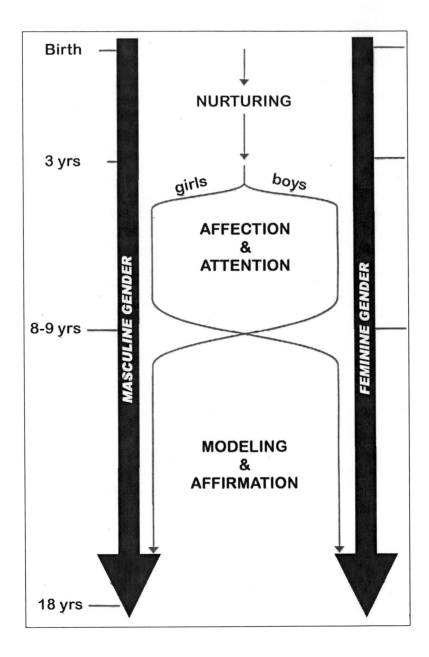

The Dysfunctional Family

Today, many children receive adequate parenting from a female parent. But with dual career families, this is changing. There are more and more children being raised by day care facilities or they are on their own...latch-key kids. However, for most children there is still some healthy female parenting through mothers or surrogates.

The major missing ingredient in parenting in contemporary culture is the Father. This lack of fathering impacts girls most in the second stage of development. Their wounds often are around distrust and hostility toward men and a hunger for affection and attention from the same men they don't trust. For the young males, the issues are tied more to the third stage; they suffer wounds from a lack of healthy modeling for their masculine identity and the encroachment of too much mothering on their internal life.

Most men in today's culture have been affected by the problem of the passive, non-involved, absentee father. The problem has created a cycle deeply engrained in the culture: Strong women marry passive men and these marriages produce strong daughters and passive sons; then the cycle repeats itself all over again. With each generation, the problems get worse and the consequences on men's masculine identity get more devastating. Today there is an epidemic of lost masculinity.

> *"When the office work and the 'information revolution' begin to dominate, the father-son bond disintegrates. If the father inhabits the house only for an hour or two in the evenings, then women's values, marvelous as they are, will be the only values in the house."*
>
> Robert Bly, <u>Iron John</u>

As home life in America has changed, so have the traditions and the ways children grow up and leave home. We live in a culture that has created a period of prolonged adolescence for most teens and young adults. This prolonged adolescence begins at puberty and ends somewhere in the twenty to thirty age bracket. But for some adults, they never seem to grow up. One of the greatest barriers many young adults have to overcome is the prolonged adolescence permitted and encouraged by our culture.

The Problem of Prolonged Adolescence

Prolonged adolescence is historically a relatively new phenomenon. Down through history, the largest majority of young people moved from childhood into adult responsibilities without having any years of irresponsible freedom to deal with. But for a variety of reasons, around the globe, primarily in the more developed industrialized countries, there has developed this period of prolonged adolescence. Interestingly, this has developed during the same period of time that a large number of fathers have been exiting family life. Individuals living in this stage of prolonged adolescence exhibit many of the problems that are directly connected to father absence and father deprivation.

Symptoms of Prolonged Adolescence:

- Acting like a spoiled dependent child when he/she doesn't get his/her way.
- Living irresponsibly, unaware of the rights and feelings of others.
- Displaying immature self-gratification: *"I want what I want now."*
- Blaming their problems on others.
- Possessing a sense of entitlement, expecting someone else to pay the bill.
- Using anger to control and manipulate others.
- Showing a lack of respect for authority: *"No one can tell me what to do."*
- Expecting someone else to clean up their messes.
- Being un-teachable, disrespectful, irreverent.
- Being self-absorbed, lacking empathy for the pain they cause.
- Believing they are bulletproof and invincible.
- Looking for someone to take care of them.
- Always searching for the easy way out.

All of these symptoms may not be observed in each individual suffering from a prolonged adolescence, but if someone exhibits several of these, it is a pretty sure bet that he has some growing up to do. There are many examples of characters like Peter Pan who never seem to grow up. These perpetually immature individuals make healthy marriages and families more difficult, if not impossible.

The absence of fathers and the lack of healthy masculine parenting are key factors to understanding how the issue of prolonged adolescence developed. Christians have been, once again, changed by the culture instead of being salt and light. Adolescence, like retirement, is not a Biblical concept and was basically unknown in the early church.

By God's design, with the onset of puberty, He has given the developing female a call into maturity that the young male does not have. The maturing process for young girls is enabled by her identification with adult women. Young males do not have comparable identification processes with adult males. They do not have a natural rite of passage as young females do.

The Concept of "Rite of Passage"

Prolonged adolescence was not an issue down through recorded history, except in the case of "privileged, spoiled rich kids." In the rural agrarian economies, teens were expected to carry their load and had little or no free time and resources for an irresponsible lifestyle. The difficulties of life conformed the youth into adult responsibilities at an earlier age than in today's world.

In ancient tribes or villages, traditions often involved older men stealing the 14 year old boys away from their mothers and taking them on a journey. Usually this event involved teaching the boys skills of war, hunting and the biological facts of life. At the end of the journey, the boys were initiated into manhood. They were endorsed by the older men and affirmed that they were no longer boys, but now warriors, men ready to fight, take a wife and start a family. Often there was some special tattoo or scar each boy received to mark him forever as a man. Sometimes he would even be given a new name by his Father to signify his entry into manhood. When he returned to the village or tribe, he returned as a man, and the mothers, family members and women received him back and celebrated him as a warrior man.

Down through history, the wisdom has been that boys cannot change into men without active intervention of older men. But in our culture, there is disrespect for elders. Older men have lost their status and are not sought out by younger males. This is a result of the devaluing of the role of father from the deprivation our culture experiences.

There were three key components to the traditional rite of passage. First, the older men were granting to the young male the permission to be a man. Secondly, they taught him the traditional skills of manhood, affirming him and training him to be a man. Thirdly, the men initiated the boy into manhood. They affirmed him in a celebration that launched him into the journey of manhood. This journey included the encouragement and reaffirmation of the young male's manhood through the daily interactions in the tribe or village.

There are no generally accepted rites of passage experiences available to the average male in contemporary culture. Boys have tried to find a benchmark: first beer, first cigarette, first sexual encounter, getting their drivers license, joining the military and so on. But there is no accepted ritual across cultures in America that affirms young males in their manhood. Gangs have rituals that are designed to initiate a boy into the gang, such as stealing, drive by shootings, or something worse. But none of these affirm the young male in his masculinity.

There are few men who understand this need the young male has for affirmation and initiation, and even fewer men who are involved enough with the boys of this culture to do the affirming or initiating. With the increase of father absent children and father deprived children, there are very few adult men who can affirm young males.

"Very few men indeed are adequately affirmed as men today, and many are pathologically split off from their masculine side altogether . . . The father who is un-affirmed in his own masculinity cannot adequately affirm the son in his."
Leanne Payne, <u>Crisis in Masculinity</u>

Until our culture recognizes the need younger males have to be initiated and affirmed and until we establish the value of wisdom and life experience of older men, it is not likely that a significant "Rite of Passage" will become the experience of the average American male.

Separation from Mother

The importance of a clean separation from Mom is a critical milestone for both female and male young adults. This separation is different for daughters than for sons.

The female child is conceived in a female womb, birthed from a female body, nursed by the female, nurtured by the female and grows up to be a female. Her development is a gender smooth path, but still when she reaches the older teen years, she needs a father figure to draw her into the world that is separate from mother.

> *"The young girl is also called up and out of infancy and girlhood and on into a fulfilling womanhood by her father's capacity to affirm her as a feminine person at each stage of her growth. In this way, he helps her separate her identity from her mother's, and he affirms her as a person in her own right. Without the father's help, the struggle is prolonged and heightened*
>
> Leanne Payne, <u>Crisis in Masculinity</u>

The male child is conceived in a female womb, birthed from a female body, nursed by the female, nurtured by the female and grows up to be a male. Without a sure break from the mother, he will struggle in a man's world and in his marriage.

> *"This (separation) is a large element in a young man being unable to accept himself as a man, as well as in male homo-sexuality, for the young lad is unable to get his identity sepa-rated from his mother, the feminine. He is barred from the necessary identification with the masculine, and his own*

masculinity goes 'begging' It is not called into life. He is un-affirmed in his gender identity."

Leanne Payne, <u>Crisis in Masculinity</u>

This separation from the nest and mother is a critical component in the developmental process. Sometimes a mother is like velcro and sometimes the teen is too scared to make the move, but eventually every child has to separate from the nest. Ideally it will be a respectful, clean break on both the mother's part and the teen's. However, when there is no father figure available to draw the young teen away from mother, and the teenager realizes that the separation from mother is going to be difficult, he/she can often resort to anger to create the separation. Dr. James Schaller says that an inappropriate mother-child development is often induced by a distant or uninvolved father. A father's presence assists both male and female young adults to make a cleaner, more respectful break from their mother.

Whatever emotional needs or issues a person has with a parent, that have not been healed, will contaminate their future adult relationships. The consequences that contaminate adult lives when the separation issue has not been clean and respectful can be seen in several ways:

Fear of Abandonment:

When a child has been too dependent on a parent figure for too long, he/she can fear separation and feeling abandoned. This carries over into their other adult relationships.

Role as Caretaker or Scapegoat:

Dr. Schaller (in <u>The Search for Lost Fathering</u>) identifies these patterns:

"When a father deserts or neglects his appropriate role, the children tend to become either caretakers or scapegoats. The caretakers love mother in ways that are beyond the child's role; they may also function as eternal baby-sitters for their siblings. Occasionally, younger children look to their older

brother or sister as the reliable 'parent,' because Mother is too emotionally crippled or just physically exhausted from playing both parental roles.

Scapegoats in the family are easy to identify. They are the ones getting into trouble in school, at work, or in their relationships. They may be called the black sheep of the family and the weight of that label hurts them a great deal."

Fear of being Smothered:

When a child has struggled to become independent from a parent figure, he can fear being smothered or controlled by another person if he gets too close in a relationship. This person may have a fear of commitment.

Marital Transferences:

When an adult has unfinished issues with a parent figure (often the parent of the opposite gender), these unfinished issues can contaminate a marriage relationship. The parent of the same gender can be a factor if he or she is too controlling and smothering. The person with unfinished issues transfers his/her emotional issues, anger and fears to the marriage partner. When these parental components enter into a marriage relationship, these interfere with intimacy, sexual freedom and often require extensive counseling and healing to be resolved.

Many men relate to their wives as if she is Mom and he is a teenage boy. Many women confess that their husbands are just like another child around the house and that she has a harder time getting him to help out with chores than she does the children. To the husband, his wife's requests or reminders seem too much like mother's instructions so he responds to them in the same passive aggressive way a teenager would.

What about "Mother Deprivation"?

We are seeing more women and men in counseling today who suffer from mother deprivation. The women find themselves caught in cultural role confusion and often lack basic skills in nurturing and mothering. Most often men who suffer from mother deprivation have a hunger for feminine attention and affection that can drive sexual issues. However, there is also clinical evidence that some issues concerning gender confusion and cross dressing are related to mother deprivation among young males. For some, dressing in female clothing is identifying with her power; for others, it is an attempt to get close to the feminine.

Clyde was a 35 year old male just released from prison for breaking and entering. He told his story that he went to prison for breaking into women's apartments to steal their underwear. He said that when he was a small boy his Mom and Dad went through an ugly divorce and that his Mom's anger was turned on him after Dad left. Since he looked just like his father he figured that was a reason for her rejection. Because the rejection was so harsh, he felt that he lost his Mom and his Dad at the same time. So, because he couldn't get close to his mother, the little six year old would sneak into her closet and get her nylon night gown or underclothes and hold these close to his face. With tears streaming down his face, he said in a little boy voice, *"That was as close as I could get to my Mommy."* Then I understood why he only broke into the apartments of middle age and older women…he was trying still to get close to his mother.

However, for both male and female children, there are many "surrogate moms" provided in our culture to alleviate some of the effects of mother deprivation. Almost all child care workers are female and early grade school teachers are usually female. Sunday Schools are almost all taught by females and many of the coaches on youth athletic teams are female. So if mother deprivation is a factor, there is some help provided. This is not true for children suffering father deprivation. There are too few men available for children suffering from father deprivation.

A Note to Single Parents
(Particularly Single Moms)

Being a single parent is possibly the most difficult job a person can do. For most single parents there are always too many details, too much scheduling, too little funds and not enough energy to go around. A parenting relationship with a father and mother who share the parenting responsibilities is by far an easier alternative. But some people do not have that option. My wife was a single Mom for 14 years raising three girls without the benefit of a spouse. I was a single parent for about five years raising my teenage son. There is not intent in this material to denigrate the hard work of single parents.

However, God's design and His ideal is that every child should have two parents, a Mom and a Dad. And the material in this book is based on that ideal. There is no intent to deny that there are many single parents raising children without the other parent who are doing an exceptional job. But the statistics gathered over the past thirty or forty years support the reality that two parents, one male and one female, provide the best environment for the healthy development of children.

Some children do well in single parent families, particularly if there is a large support system from other family members or even from non-family members such as relationships within a church or close friends. Many single parents are not single parents by choice... they were left to parent alone by death, divorce, or desertion, but they are alone and doing the best they can under those circumstances. If their children were asked and if adults who were raised in single parent homes were asked, most would tell you that they wish they had had both a father and mother.

In this material we focus on the wounds children suffer and how these wounds contaminate the lives and relationships of their adult lives when the parenting they experienced is skewed by father absence, father abuse or father deprivation. <u>We are not blaming their parents,</u> we are addressing what is the reality of the life experiences of millions of adults who grew up in dysfunctional homes. Some single parent homes can be more functional than two parent homes.

Our desire is to help these wounded people find God's healing touch and a deeper understanding of His love and mercy toward them. Our prayer is that He would use this material to accomplish His purposes in each reader's life.

The lost ingredient in families is healthy fathering. Possibly as high as 80% of all American adults suffer from some degree of father deprivation from their childhood and a large percentage of adults experienced father absence in childhood.

How did our society become fatherless?
Where did all the fathers go?

CHAPTER FIVE

Where Did All the Fathers Go?

Many forces have combined to undermine the role of the father and authentic masculinity in America and around the world. Since this is not a sociology book, it is not within our scope to detail all the factors that have undermined fathering in the American family. We will only skim the surface of the more obvious issues.

Shift in the Culture

In the last 300 years the United States has experienced a major culture transition. In the late 1700's and early 1800's, the American way of life was primarily rural with 97% of all families living in rural areas. Fathers primarily worked the land. They were home most days during the daylight hours, and most nights they slept in the same house with their children. Just being in the presence of the father enabled the young male to "catch" masculinity and learn what men do. Before the Industrial Revolution, a son hung out with his father, felt his presence and learned how to do what men did. Today that culture has vanished; things have been reversed.

The 97% rural and agrarian way of life has shifted and is now 96% urban. Fathers, trying to care for their families, learned in the late 1800's that factories paid more per week than they could make on the farms and ranches in a month. So to provide for the family, they began to work daylight hours in the factories of America. The mother and children were left to take care of the land and the animals. But most fathers were still able to be at home some hours most nights if they lived near a factory. For other fathers, they lived in the city where the factories were located and tried to get home on weekends. Eventually many relocated their families to the cities.

Sales oriented careers were introduced and early door-to-door salesmen began to travel the streets and highways of America. Many fathers were now on the road and not at home with their families at nights. This trend still takes many fathers away from their families so that many mothers have to function as single parents most days of the week. There are large numbers of weekend fathers in America today.

Then the information industry was born. More men traveled and worked in IT professions or as consultants. Even those that were home at nights began to bring work home with them. Children began to feel less and less important. Now the local economy has become a global economy and work takes more and more parents, both men and women, out of the home many evenings during a month.

Change in Family Support

Another aspect of this shift from agrarian to urban culture has been the change in the size of the American family and the support available from the extended family. Large families with six or more children have given way to smaller families with all the children close to each other in age. The family support system of grandparents, older siblings, aunts and uncles who often lived in close proximity has disappeared. The average young couple in America today does not have the support of extended families so they are forced to function as a small isolated family cell, depending on strangers for emotional support and child care.

Day Care has become an expensive reality as more and more women enter the work force. Children are in the care of "trained" child care workers who perform necessary duties, but often lack the warmth and love of a parent or relative.

This major shift in family structure also removed the male relatives who could serve as surrogate fathers from the support system of the family. And most Day Care or Mother's Day Out programs in local churches are staffed by female staff, so there are no surrogate father figures available for the average child. This is also true of the public schools and the Sunday School programs of the average church. There are precious few surrogate father figures available in children's lives until they get into the upper grades of school or competitive athletics. Even Cub Scouts have Den Mothers; many athletic teams for younger children are now being coached by women because there are no fathers available to lead and coach.

Effects of War

War takes fathers out of a society. Millions were lost in the two World Wars. During three different battles in World War I, over one million men were killed in each battle. On D Day in World War II, over 200,000 thousand men died. In the Viet Nam war some 54,000 men were killed and thousands of vets were crippled by wounds of the body and soul. Wars across the world have taken entire generations of men away from their families. Since 9-11, and including that terrible day, many more have given their lives. When you consider the impact of these deaths, children are the ones that suffer most without a father. Entire countries have lost generations of fathers.

And there are wars on the streets of America. Most of the victims of crime, the drug war, addictions such as alcoholism, gang violence and so on are men; men who could have been fathers. A lot of fathers have been killed as policemen, firemen and other law enforcement officers. More men die in industrial accidents, car wrecks and suicides. All of these issues have robbed American children of men who could have been fathers.

Effects of the Sexual Revolution

The new found sexual freedom in America has also robbed children of fathers. The divorce rate among couples is above 50%, even in church groups. Unwed births now are 65% in some racial groups and approaching 50% of all births in America. Couples are choosing to live together instead of marrying, and many times kids are caught in the mysterious land of *"Who is this new guy living with Mom?"* The real victims of the Sexual Revolution are the children who have lost a stable home life so that Mom and Dad can experience sexual freedom.

Pornography is an epidemic; as many as 50% of men in some areas struggle with addiction to internet porn. Many children as young as eight or nine years of age have unintentionally been exposed to and traumatized by sexually graphic details on the web. Pornography is now a multibillion dollar business and growing daily. Many men turn to porn because it is an "easier" way to find sexual stimulation, not realizing that it is a progressive addiction that can lead to crimes such as rape, molestation and even murder. Research with convicted child molesters and rapists has found that pornography is a factor in their evolution.

The divorce rate has leveled off, but there are signs that many women are opting out of marriage because of pornography, adultery or other sexual issues, and many women have turned to lesbian relationships as valid alternatives.

We are now forty or more years into the sexual revolution, and American society is experiencing a crisis in sexual sanity, child abuse, rape, and masculinity. Many men are feeling lost, isolated, misunderstood and emasculated. More and more women are feeling like sex objects and fear that heterosexual relationships are too confusing and too difficult. Some have concluded *"Who needs a man anyway?"*

While he was a senior psychiatrist at the Menninger Foundation in Topeka, Kansas, Harold M. Voth, M.D. wrote in his book <u>The Castrated Family</u>, a summary of what he believed to be a critical problem facing American families.

> *"Far-reaching and serious consequences result when internal family arrangements deviate from the norm. Virtually every patient I have personally treated, or whose treatment I have studied through a research endeavor, has revealed an aberrant family constellation. The most common pattern was the family in which the mother was domineering and aggressive and the father was weak and passive. Some of these fathers were aggressive and assertive in their work situations but timid and weak in relation to their wives. The wives in these marriages clearly 'wore the pants'. Another pattern was that of a weak mother who tended to cling to her children, and a tyrannical father who was dictatorial but incapable of experiencing closeness to his wife or children. While it may seem that such a father is head of the family, actually much of the responsibility and authority falls to the wife except for periods when the father makes his presence felt by angry, usually irrational, outbursts. Some women are forced to fill the role of both mother and father by necessity. These women may be feminine, but the absence of the father places all of the responsibilities on them; the effects of this family pattern on children as well as on themselves are not good."*

While new family patterns are increasing today, the cycle of stronger mothers and passive or non-involved fathers is deeply ingrained in several generations of families in America. Changing cultural patterns are difficult and require intentional choices by the individuals involved. Recognizing the need to change is the first step.

Unfortunately, the Christian Church, for many reasons, has lost its influence over the majority of men. Most men do not think of the church as a place for training or help with fathering or with father wounds. They have no concept that they are to be representatives of the Heavenly Father to their children. Until the contemporary church addresses this issue, it is unlikely it will be a significant influence in this culture. A feminized church appealing to domesticated males and strong women will never significantly impact the world.

If the contemporary church becomes the authority on Father Love and begins to challenge men to step up and take on the mantle of the noble role of being an earthly father, then we can anticipate that men will again show up and suit up as fathers. This is the prayer many Christians have been praying.

It is unrealistic to think that the cultural shift from rural/agrarian to urban will ever shift back. It is also unlikely that the large extended family support system will ever return. But it is possible for us to learn from these long-gone cultural patterns the importance of supportive relationships and to create new support systems. It is possible for neighbors, friends, and church groups to learn how to connect on a deeper emotional level so that trust can be built that would enable families to support other families. These extended "family-style" support systems could best be built around an organization like a church, but it is possible that neighbors and friends can learn to cooperate with one another to create a "support system of choice" for mutual well-being.

We must restore healthy masculine energy to the parenting equation. Ideally, a husband-wife coalition is the best parenting culture, but surrogate fathering can be much better than a "no father" kind of culture.

Healthy fathering is a required ingredient of healthy personality and soul development. Children need Dads to help them be prepared for what the world throws at them.

CHAPTER SIX

Men and Father Deprivation

The lack of a warm, loving, affectionate father figure has a great impact on a boy's life. The impact of father-deprivation affects the young male most significantly between the ages of ten and adult. The major emotional impact is in the third stage of development when the young boy is looking for a male role model.

Many of the issues and problems men have can be understood as scars from father deprivation. The lack of fathering affects the young male most during the adolescent years when he is working to develop his masculine identity. The lack of a meaningful relationship with the male parent undermines a boy's self-esteem and confidence as he is trying to understand and be what a real man is. This lack of a healthy male model puts the developing adolescent at a distinct disadvantage as he ventures into the adult world.

> *"We live in a father-hungry culture, so how can a boy imagine what it's like to be a man?"*
>
> Robert Bly, <u>Iron John</u>

Where does the young male define his masculinity when his father is abusive, non-involved, too remote or gone altogether? Too often these young males look to mother or underneath a woman's skirt to try and find their manhood. The media shows few healthy masculine role models, and there are few surrogate fathers available.

A young boy, trying to understand his sexual identity, is faced with the most devastating wounds and consequences of father deprivation. They include:

- Poor Masculine Self Esteem
- Lack of Affirmation in Masculine Role
- Difficulty in connecting with other Un-affirmed Males
- Fear of the Feminine
- Vulnerability to Addictions
- Sexual Problems
- Difficulty Controlling Anger
- Contaminated God Image
- No Role Model for Healthy Fathering
- Career and Work Related Difficulties

Wound #1: Poor Masculine Self-Esteem

A boy with an ineffective father relationship grows up with a poor sense of masculinity. He has little confidence in himself as a man. Since he lacked an effective relationship with his Dad, he does not really know how to be a man. When the young male is not connected to his father emotionally and does not have a healthy male role model, his masculine self-esteem is usually wounded and un-affirmed. Typically these men feel the need to prove their masculinity (that they are "real men").

The need to prove he is a real man is buried so deep in his unconscious that he is not aware of how it drives him. It is the pressure to perform, to prove himself, to live up to some "masculine ideal". He drives himself endlessly trying to be what he imagines a real man to be. But in his compulsive work habits, there is a lack of personal confidence that he has what it takes, that he is as good as the next guy. He has little sense that he is okay.

These young men become vulnerable to the world's false ideas and lies about masculinity. These lies and false ideas are called "Masculine Myths."

Un-affirmed males utilize their emotional energy to prove what they are not, instead of being who they are. It is an interesting paradox, but he is determined that no one will see him as feminine, dependent, emotional, passive, fearful, helpless, a failure, a loser, or impotent. It is like the proverbial squirrel cage. Since he can never sufficiently prove to himself and others what he is not, he burns himself out, running around and around in the cage, trying to prove he is a "man". The self loathing and humiliation, when he feels he is not man enough, overwhelm him.

Cultural pressures on young males, to behave in traditionally masculine ways, have been great over the years. The pressures on the young female are not as great. It is fine for a girl to be considered a "Tomboy", but for a young male to be a "Sissy" was and is a horrible insult.

The Christian world view, based on Biblical understanding, can help men struggling with their masculine identity. Christian men have as their role model Jesus and, as their model for fathering, the Heavenly Father. Because of the Biblical image of Jesus and the Heavenly Father, healthy Christianity can teach a healthy, authentic picture of masculinity. When healthy men embrace Christianity and band together, they become a strong support system that can help younger men avoid the world's myths about what it means to be a man. But unfortunately, too many men without a Christian support system, or even sometimes with one, walk into the minefield which is made up of the world's myths.

MYTH as defined in the American Heritage Dictionary:

"A real or fictional story, recurring theme, or character type that appeals to the consciousness of a people by embodying its cultural ideals or by giving expression to deep, commonly felt emotions."

Contemporary culture, through masculine myths, has hung a major definition problem on men. Men do not know how to define authentic masculinity. What is a "real man"? No concept has gotten more boys into trouble than this one of trying to be a "real man." He is told all his life to *"Grow up and be a man,"* but no one has ever told him what that would look like. If and when he did make it, who would be there to tell him: *"Good Job! Now you are a real man."*

Men are confused about what it means to be a man. Everything has changed. Most men recognize that the old world is gone forever much like the dinosaur, but what are men to be like in the new world? Is there any concept such as "authentic masculinity" that is relevant for all worlds and all cultures? Sociologists, biologists and anthropologists, who work from an evolutionary pre-supposition, would likely argue that all such concepts are irrelevant in the on-going process of evolution. They would say that everything changes, particularly with families, gender roles and the way human beings relate to each other. The roles that survive are the roles that matter.

Without understanding that there is a loving Heavenly Father and a big brother role model in Jesus, the secular world offers little to help men. The more wounded these men are from their families of origin, the more vulnerable they are to these myths.

Dysfunctional families have left young men wounded and vulnerable to these "urban legends" about what makes a male a "real man". Their wounds have caused men to struggle with who they are and how they become a "real man" if they ever figure out what a "real man" is.

Myth #1: A "real man" is a rugged individualist.

In a crisis, a "real man" pulls himself together to fight for survival (i.e. Indiana Jones, John Wayne, Audie Murphy, Clint Eastwood, Charles Bronson, James Bond, Iron Man, Jason Bourne, etc.) If he is to survive, he must do it himself.

Sylvester Stallone set out on the mission to change the image of males in the movies. He said, *"Screen characters seem more like young ladies than real men, and it's time to re-establish the balance."* (John Mellen, Big Bad Wolves). Stallone gave us Rocky Balboa and Rambo as two of the great icons to "rugged individualism."

Myth #2: A "real man" is non-emotional.

Men are taught from early in life to deny and repress feelings. The young boy is told to stop crying. His father says, *"Hush that crying or I will give you something to cry about."* So feelings become unknown and unpredictable. Emotions and feelings are a currency women deal in and the young man is fearful he will become vulnerable if he lingers with his feelings too long.

In our current culture the popularity of "extreme sports" and horrific scary movies represent some of the more dramatic ways young men seek to find their feelings. An adrenaline rush may be the closest thing to a real feeling many have experienced. The same could be said for rodeos, fast cars, one night stands and other risk taking behaviors.

Policemen, firemen, and EMT workers, men who are expected to do the risky, tough jobs, have to maintain control of their feelings. American soldiers coming home from Iraq and fighting terrorists are suffering post-traumatic stress at an increasingly high rate. If such a diagnosis was available during the earlier conflicts (i.e. WW I and WW II) we would have seen thousands of veterans diagnosed with similar PTSD symptoms. No human being can experience the horrors of war without some consequences from such traumas.

In our culture, the adrenaline rush, anger and sexual feelings seem to be the only feelings "real men" can acknowledge.

Myth #3: A "real man" is always in control.

It is often humorous when we observe some of these myths and the way they are worked out in our lives and in the lives of men who we know. For example, have you ever thought of the pets men choose? Men will usually choose a dog over a cat because he can't control a cat. He can teach a dog to do lots of things, but he can't get a cat to do what he wants, ever! Another example concerns men and why they won't stop and ask directions. How long will a man drive around looking for a destination before he will stop and ask for directions? Maybe the invention of the GPS will take care of all that!

If a man is not in control, he must act like he is in control. Often men turn to anger to try to gain control when they feel frightened which may be a key to understanding violence in male-female relationships (i.e. *"I couldn't get her to shut up!"*).

Myth #4: A "real man" achieves worth by performance, accomplishments, etc.

Men look to their external accomplishments and achievements to feel good about themselves. Many fathers reinforce this when the boys are young. A boy earns Dad's accolades by being the best, faster, stronger than other boys. How many fathers, for their personal self worth, have coached and cheered their sons through youth sports leagues? On any given Saturday you can find fathers and grandfathers stroking their egos on the athletic fields while their son beats another man's son. This is one root behind much of the work ethic and workaholic personality that so many men buy into in today's world. Men feel a need to beat the other guy. It also is a reason that sports dominate so many men's lives.

Myth #5: A "real man" must always win.

This myth is closely tied to the previous one. The emphasis on competition clearly demonstrates the belief that is communicated to young boys: *"If I beat you, whether it is in football, boxing, or tiddly winks, I am a better man than you are!"*

When men get too old to compete on the athletic field, they often choose teams and place bets. The guy who picks the winner is the better man. The multi-million dollar gambling business is built on old athletes and wannabes who are still trying to win (i.e. fantasy football, office pools, etc.).

Myth #6: A "real man" is rarely sick and is able to handle as much pain as possible.

He is not supposed to let anyone know how bad he is hurting. Men consciously and unconsciously neglect and ignore their bodies. In marriage, his wife often has to be the "keeper of his body" as he gets older. Any male who played contact sports as a child will remember the coach's comments to an injured player: *"You're not hurt! There's no bone sticking out, get back out there!"*

And many young men play all sorts of games to prove to themselves that they are tough enough. G. Gordon Liddy, one of the Watergate figures, said, *"Once I held my hand in the flame of a candle...just to see how tough I was."* A young Marine was showing some of the men in one of our Man 2.0 groups the games he and his buddies played with lit cigarettes, holding them in their hands, their mouths, and in the crease of their folded arms to demonstrate how rugged and tough they were. The scars proved his story.

Myth #7: A "real man" always succeeds and performs well sexually.

Success and winning even in sex is seen as proof he is a real man. He has to always be ready and he must perform every time the opportunity presents itself. The number of women he seduces is a means of keeping score.

Myth #8: A "real man" hunts and fishes and engages in outdoor activities with other men.

To be a real man, he has to own several guns, hunt deer and birds and be a good fisherman. Road trips, to engage in these activities with other "real men", confirm he has arrived.

Myth #9: A "real man" is a great athlete.

Real men are athletes. The only other type of men are wimps. The older he gets the better he was and he loves to get together with old team mates and reminisce.

Myth #10: A "real man" is successful financially.

Finances and personal wealth are the score cards for the "real man". Making the big score drives men thinking that true success is financial success.

Myth #11: A "real man" never allows a woman to have control over him.

By the time the average male is 12 or 13, he has had all the feminine control and input he wants in his life. When a father is not present, mothers have to take charge. Out of love, she tries to direct and influence her son's life. The more intrusive and forceful she is, the more likely her son will openly rebel.

Many of the problems we see in marriage conflicts can be traced back to this need to be in control and the male's inability to deal with a wide range of intense feelings. However, we must also acknowledge the role of the male hormone testosterone in all of these issues.

The Role of Testosterone:

Testosterone is a factor in the conflict with Mom and in all of these myths young males buy into to try to prove their masculinity.

In his book <u>Men and Marriage</u>, George Gilder writes:

"The man is rendered more aggressive, exploratory, volatile, competitive and dominant, more visual, abstract, and impulsive, more muscular, appetitive, and tall. He is less nurturant, moral, domestic, stable and peaceful, less auditory, verbal, and sympathetic, less durable, healthy, and dependable, less balanced, and less close to the ground. He is more compulsive sexually and less secure. The culprit is testosterone."

Here are a few things to remember about the male hormone:

- Testosterone cycles every 20 minutes.
- Testosterone levels are highest in the Fall.
- Levels of testosterone are the highest in the mornings.
- Testosterone causes men to be:

    o More aggressive.
    o More competitive.
    o More dominant.
    o More exploratory.
    o More volatile.
    o More muscular/tall.

God never intended for a single Mom to ride herd on a testosterone loaded 16 year old by herself. Rogue masculine energy needs male supervision to teach younger men the need for controls and responsibility in dealing with their testosterone. Without healthy role models of masculinity, these boys are vulnerable to the world's strategies, ideas and all the myths that destroy their lives, families and friendships. It is time for men to recognize what is happening to their sons and to younger men. The time to stand up and fight to change the situation is now.

Wound #2: Lack of Affirmation in Masculine Role

A young man, going through a painful divorce, sits in my office and begins to cry. *"I don't know how to get a job, keep a job or how to have a relationship. I don't know how to face life and I have no one to tell me how to do it."*

Another man confesses the pain of having no father and to a deep subterranean anger that is triggered at certain times. He thinks it is anger at being left alone in the world. *"I have felt alone all my whole life."* As he talked about his anger, he began to describe the latest incident in which he lost control. He said, *"I think I felt bullied. I was bullied as a kid and I didn't have anyone to tell me how to deal with it."*

This is the world in which too many young males live. John Eldredge writes about a kind of loneliness that pisses off so many of these young men: *"I'll tell you why I'm hacked. There are two reasons. First, I'm hacked because there's no one here to show me how to do this. Why do I always have to figure this stuff out on my own?"* He then says, *"I'm also hacked because I can't do it myself, mad that I need help. Long ago I resolved to live without needing help..."*

In these brief scenarios you see a picture of the inner frustration of thousands of men, men who feel like little boys on the inside trying really hard to not be like their fathers; men who do not feel comfortable in their own skin. You hear their anger and you see their inner vow to never ask for help, to never appear needy. These reactions are all triggered by father deprivation...the aloneness that isolates men from men everywhere. Nothing angers a man any faster than his feeling humiliated because he can't do what other men can. *"If only my father had been here, my life might have been different. It isn't fair!"* Such are the issues roaming around in the mind and life of the un-affirmed male.

Several behavioral responses develop from this lack of affirmation and men typically use one or more of these five ways to compensate.

(1) **Control (often resorting to anger):** Un-affirmed males often respond defensively to anyone who challenges their control or questions them in their decisions.

(2) **Status (often resorting to being a poser):** The male who has the most perceived status, whether it is a job title, degrees or honors is seen by these un-affirmed peers as the "better" man. It is interesting that these men seem to prefer titles much more so than their female counterparts.

(3) **Material Possessions (often resorting to incurring debt):** The man who makes the bigger pay check or who has the more expensive toys in his garage or whose wife has the most diamonds is seen as the better man. The big house, the expensive car and the appearance of material success are the key. Why do you think there are so many men buying "knock-off" versions of Rolex watches and expensive pens?

(4) **Competition (often resorting to gambling and cheating):** From childhood, boys are taught that winning is everything, and the one who wins is the best man. The man who wins at love, war, football, cards, or whatever is the best man.

(5) **Sexual Conquests (often unable to stop acting out even after marriage):** The man who makes it with the most women is seen as the best man. This issue underlies many stories that men share in the locker room, whether they are true or the figment of their collective imaginations.

James Bond is a symbol of the true male hero for many men. He has great status and plenty of money. He always wins and hooks up with at least one beautiful woman before the movie ends. So, in some secret fantasy, young males imagine themselves not being incompetent or failures, but rather being the super hero.

It is an interesting contrast to consider these five strategies men use to prove their masculinity and the life of Jesus. Jesus did not exercise any of these strategies and He remains the greatest man who ever walked the earth.

Wound #3: Trouble Connecting with other Un-affirmed Males

A common scar that many un-affirmed males carry is a hunger for masculine relationships, yet an inability to develop and feel comfortable with other men. Since his Dad did not relate to him, he has no concept of male-to-male interaction. Often these fathers had no close male friends of their own so they could not serve as models for their sons.

A lot of men know how to "do" things with other men, like hunting, fishing, sports, etc. But they do not know how to interact or relate on a feeling level. Often "doing" replaces "relating". After they have talked about the weather, the cute new secretary, the latest sporting event or similar topics, they have very little to discuss.

Their stories are often third person accounts and reveal very little about the man himself. Emotions and feelings are rarely, if ever, shared with another male and certainly in this culture, touching, such as hugging, etc. is considered taboo off the athletic field. On the field they can "high five," "knuckle knock," slap butts and even hug, but off the field they barely shake hands.

Adult males in our culture are, for the most part, lonely and demonstrate a lack of close male relationships. If you ask the average man who his best friend is, most will respond *"My wife."* Others will talk about an old college chum who they haven't talked to in three years or longer. The reality is that most men do not have a close male friend.

Many men see their need for friendship as a weakness or a hold-over from adolescence. But when, years later, they run into an old army buddy or an old college friend, they are overjoyed and realize somewhere deep inside what they have missed.

Unfortunately the most isolated males are often the married ones. They will all say their wives are their best friends and they blame their lack of close male buddies on the fact that they are too busy with work, kids etc. Probably the real reasons are a lot more complex. Wives need to understand, men need other men to encourage them and support them with their struggles in life. It is important to have a good relationship with one's wife, but often a man burns out or wipes out if he does not have a support system of healthy masculine energy in his life.

Men who never connected with their fathers have difficulty in relationships with other men. They did not learn from their fathers how men relate. They have never had anyone teach them about such connections. In addition they have a desire for male contact, like a child wanting Daddy's attention and affection, but they fear letting anyone know they have such a desire. They fear being labeled gay or queer or whatever name his peers might saddle him with. Such teasing is a very common male bonding devise, but for many young males this is a painful learning process. Peers can be cruel out of their own insecurities.

In the early to mid-nineties there was a men's movement that broke out across the country. A number of Wild Man Workshops were held and men talked about a new kind of male who could have relationships and be open and vulnerable. There may be some fragments around, but for all practical effect, it is dead. For the most part this movement never broke into the church.

However, across America today there is a new movement among men within the Christian world who are discovering what Jesus meant when He said, *"By the way you love one another the world will know that you are my disciples."* John 13:34-35).

Wound #4: Fear of the Feminine

Another wound and scar that males deprived of emotionally effective fathering manifest has to do with their inability to relate to

90

women. Most of these males had adequate mothering in the first ten years of life. By the time they begin to approach puberty, they are ready for masculine input. If there is not a father figure available for boys to relate to, Moms try to fill the gap. She tries to meet the needs that a Dad should be meeting.

Women, who are trying to be father and mother both, are seeking to compensate for the emotionally non-involved father figure. They are trying to make up for the absence or passivity of the father. The stronger, more dominant, intrusive and smothering the mothers become, the greater the boy's hostility and bitterness become even though mother's intentions are usually good.

Mothers become the objects of ambivalent feelings in their sons. These young men may admire, respect and even spend lots of energy protecting her, yet there are often feelings of anger and destructive rage seething just below the surface at what the sons perceive as controlling, smothering behavior. He would never want to hurt her, but he may vow to get away from her attentions, emotionally and physically, as soon as possible. Distance, emotionally and personally, becomes a good means of protecting the young man from her dominance. This distancing can become a tactic that he uses in numerous relationships with the opposite sex. Too often, unfinished issues with Mom contaminate marriages.

In adulthood the roots of a boy's anger, even rage, towards his mother are displaced to other women. Hostility toward women is coupled with the fear of being dominated by a woman. He may vow, unconsciously, that he will never allow another woman to control his life like his mother did. Often this is not a conscious fear, but shows up in the ways a man avoids closeness or intimacy with women.

When a man fears being controlled or smothered by a woman, he may choose to make her a sex object. Erotic closeness is the only intimacy that he can trust to keep her from dominating him. In his mind, if he makes her a sex object he knows what to do with her.

In marriage, these men often displace fears of control and smothering from their mothers onto their wives. The husbands become compliant and silent or they may become angry and distant. Whichever way they behave, their unconscious strategy is to nullify the attempts of female control.

Research studies have found that men suffering father depriva-tion mixed with strong mothering have difficulty in forming lasting heterosexual relationships. They have unstable courtship relation-ships. Studies revealed a high degree of dependence on mother, even after marriage, among men whose fathers died when they were young.

Again, many young males grew up with too little fathering and too much mothering. By the time a young male is 10 or 11 years old, he has had all the mothering he wants. He is ready for masculine input. But often anger and fear become factors in his attempts to deal with women. The anger and hostility toward women is directly related to the intrusiveness and dominance of the mother figure in a boy's life. Due to the imbalance between the masculine and femi-nine energy in the family of origin, he grows up determined to never allow a woman to have the control and power over him that his Mother did.

These issues have a greater detrimental effect on marriage than most men and women ever realize. These are the issues that fuel marital transferences. Since many men find it necessary to always appear in control and try to deny their feelings, it should be apparent that these behaviors hinder intimate, close relationships.

Often men are taught early in life that it is not good for them to be close and intimate, so in their adult lives they are inept and uncomfortable in relationships. To handle their lives, they detach themselves from any relationship that might provoke any uncontrol-lable feeling / response. He becomes comfortable in denying any neediness: *"I don't need you." "I'm not angry." "I don't feel like crying."* Because feelings are the realm of the feminine, he does not permit free expression and exerts controls over himself. He becomes a "poser," a facade of what he really is. He controls himself by denying his feelings.

When men deny their true feelings, they lose their negative feel-ings as well as their positive feelings. When a man blocks his anger, he also blocks his empathy to some degree. You cannot block one emotion without having all of your emotions impacted. When this denial occurs, men begin to lose their strength and their ability to deal with conflict. They are often unable to set healthy boundaries.

On some unconscious level, men often deny their true feelings so they can relate to the women in their lives.

The Soft Male Phenomena:

When the masculine role models are effectively removed from a culture and mothers take charge, young males tend to develop a more feminized form of masculinity.

> *"As men begin to examine women's history and women's sensibility, some men begin to notice what was called their feminine side and pay attention to it. There is something wonderful about this development- I mean the practice of men welcoming their own feminine consciousness and nurturing it...and yet I have the sense that there is something wrong. The male in the past twenty years has become more thoughtful and more gentle. But by this process he has not become more free. He's a nice boy who pleases not only his mother but also the young woman he is living with- but many of these men are not happy. You quickly notice the lack of energy in them. They are life-preserving but not exactly life-giving."*
>
> Robert Bly, <u>Iron John</u>

Today there are a large number of men who fit the "soft male" description. Charles was in his late twenties. He worked in the manufacture of computer chips. He came for counseling because of his conflicts with the young women in his life. His self-esteem was closely enmeshed to the way these women responded to him. He had developed a major drinking problem to try to handle his pain. As his story unraveled in therapy, his family of origin was a tale of divorce, a biological father who deserted the family and a step-father who was abusive to Charles, his mother and family. Charles's words dripped with anger. He suffered from father deprivation and he was one of the "soft males" that Robert Bly talked about. He found his sensitive "feminine side" because he did not want to be anything like his biological father or the abusive step-father he had known. He turned from the masculinity he had seen modeled to a gentler version that had robbed him of much of his power and passion for life. Charles was stuck somewhere between adolescence and adult mature masculinity.

These men are referred to by other men as "domesticated," "castrated," "whipped, "no balls", etc. Most men see them as allowing women and the feminine to dominate their lives. Some of these men may be gay, but most are heterosexuals that don't want to have conflict with women. These soft males have concluded that the old ways of proving masculinity...sex, power, anger, control, money and cars...don't seem to work anymore. Unfortunately, many institutions and organizations, including the average church in America, have become controlled by and dominated by a coalition of strong women and soft males.

Wound #5: Vulnerability to Addictions

The grief and emotional pain men carry as the result of their father deprivation is tremendous, and cultural myths cause many men to keep their feelings bottled-up. Addictions are a way to deaden this pain, distract themselves from it or cope with it. Often, a major part of the male bonding process involves risk taking behaviors (adrenaline) and addictive substances (alcohol, drugs, nicotine, etc.). Since some of these behaviors are considered by many young males as rites of passage into real manhood, the young male can slide very easily into addictions. Many men are walking addictions just waiting to break out.

These men are burying their pain under counterfeit comforts. Instead of bringing the pain to God for comfort and healing, they use counterfeit comforts which can lead to addictions, despair and even sometimes an early death.

Wound #6: Sexual Difficulties

Typically acting out sexually at the earliest possible opportunity is another rite of passage for young males. It is a way of proving his masculinity and demonstrating to his buddies he has what it takes. But really it is more the young male trying to prove to himself that he is a real man.

He turns to the feminine to get comfort just like he did as a young boy wanting Mommy to kiss his scratched knee and make it better. Men try to crawl under a woman's skirt to find comfort and a sense of being a real man. He is looking for his masculine strength and power in the wrong places. Men need to get close to other men in non-sexual ways. It is only through the masculine that the masculine can be acquired.

These same men, after they get married, discover that their sexual appetite changes. Because of unfinished issues with their mothers, they often have difficulty finding their wives sexually appealing. This is another example of marital transference. Their wife becomes more like a parent figure than a romantic peer relationship. In their later years, after age fifty or so, many men find their interest in sexual activity with their wives disappearing or totally gone.

Wound #7: Difficulty Controlling Anger

Anger has become a major factor in understanding and dealing with men. Because of the wounds men experience, many have hurts, fears and shame that they cover over or hide with their anger. So many males are carrying father wounds that an epidemic of anger is sweeping our society. In cities across America, the major freeways are war zones and workplaces have become dangerous environments. Even in small towns, young people fear violence from their peers and every week it seems another teen commits homicide. Schools from coast to coast are under siege from angry kids and belligerent parents. Anger that turns violent is everyday fare. No one is safe from the possibility of violence.

Anger is a universal experience. Everyone gets angry at times and anyone can be either the object of another person's anger or an observer of explosive rage. Christians are not exempt. We have even seen examples of violence played out in some churches here in America. In many areas of the world, Christians are victims of numerous verbal and other expressions and consequences of anger encountered daily. Anger truly is a common human ailment.

Anger was designed by God to be a secondary survival emotion, originally meant to protect humans from predators and natural enemies. Anger is a protective emotion that is aroused when a person is frightened or hurt. A person walks into a dark room. Suddenly someone jumps out. The unsuspecting person first experiences fear from the surprise, but the fear can quickly become anger, even if it is a friendly prank. Likewise when a person gets hurt, his anger rises as a self-protective measure.

Anger is God's gift to humans to be used to protect a person from hurt or from something that frightens him. God intended it to be used to protect and defend the vulnerable, the helpless, the young and the righteous. Anger works like a suit of armor to protect the individual and serves a powerful, useful purpose when it is expressed appropriately. Anger was never intended to be used to manipulate, control, dominate or abuse other people. Anger, when expressed appropriately, is helpful; but when it is used inappropriately, it becomes hurtful and destructive. The danger arises when anger is not dealt with, but suppressed or repressed over a period of time. Anger becomes dangerous when it is stored and stockpiled like a nuclear arsenal, just waiting for the right triggering event.

There are several reasons why anger is a major problem for males, including Christians:

- Anger always precedes violence. Violence never occurs without the presence of a stockpile of old unexpressed anger.
- Anger cancels out a person's concern for consequences. An angry person explodes without considering what the effect of his behaviors might be on other people. The stockpiled anger can quickly become rage with no thought given to possible consequences.
- Anger undermines a person's ability to trust others. Angry people are always on the defensive. They are hyper-vigilant, expecting and waiting for someone to cross them.

- <u>Anger is a learning disability</u>. Stockpiled anger creates an inability and an unwillingness to learn. Learning is a taking in process, much like swallowing; anger is just the opposite. New information cannot be received because the angry person is too busy spitting out. A person can't spit and swallow at the same time!
- <u>Anger contaminates the communication process</u>. An angry person is not able to hear what the other person is saying. Stockpiled anger can work as well as earplugs!
- <u>Anger causes a person to misinterpret and distort his environment</u>. Stockpiled anger gets generalized and transferred from past experiences and relationships, causing a person to misinterpret or misread another's intentions. A current angry situation can serve as a trigger to release old stored up anger on an unsuspecting person. And the scary part is that no one knows how big the other guy's stockpile of anger may be. Most road rage in our culture is this type of experience.
- <u>Anger stirs up anger in other people</u>. If anger is like a spark, stockpiled anger is like gasoline. Anger provokes fear in the individual it is focused on; it requires lots of maturity to not react to anger with anger.
- <u>Anger gives Satan an opportunity (foothold) in a Christian's life</u>. Paul instructed his followers to not let the sun go down on their anger (Eph. 4:26) giving the enemy the opportunity to drag them down.
- <u>The anger of man does not accomplish the purposes of God</u> (James 1:20).

Remember anger is a secondary emotion. It is always preceded by some experience that is hurtful or fearful, whether that experience is a physical threat or an emotional hurt or humiliation. Anger becomes a coping device for a young male in any situation when he feels challenged, made fun of or when he feels out of control. The experience of being humiliated is one of the worst emotional pains for a male; it can trigger terrible anger as he reacts to prove he is a real man and will not be toyed with.

As noted earlier in the book, testosterone makes young males more aggressive, more volatile, more dominant and competitive. Young men, who carry father wounds, often use anger in ways that are destructive and hurtful to themselves and the people who are close to them. An inappropriate expression or use of anger, without a healthy father figure or male influence to set boundaries and controls on these young males, can be a hazard in society. Remember the most accurate predictor of crime in any neighborhood is the number of fatherless homes in that neighborhood.

Even in nature we can see examples of testosterone without boundaries and controls.

The rogue elephant issue:

Rogue elephants are vicious and destructive elephants that separate from the herd and roam alone. Game wardens in Africa became aware of the significant number of young rogue elephants in certain herds of elephants. A study was conducted to determine what the problem was. They discovered that poachers were killing the older male elephants for their ivory and leaving the herd without the strength and wisdom of the older bulls to keep the younger bulls in check. As they researched it further, they found that young elephants would become rogues whenever there was no older male elephant to be the model and coach to keep them in line.

Something similar happens among humans. Again, it was never intended for a mother to have to rein in a testosterone loaded 16 year old by herself. Fathers are needed to model, coach and keep the young males in line so they don't become rogues like the young elephants.

A similar phenomenon was observed in Omaha, Nebraska. A group of mainly African-American men became concerned about the rogue males forming gangs and dominating their neighborhoods with drugs and violence. So the fathers formed a group in 1989 called MAD DADS. Several of these Dads began to hang out in the neighborhood and walk the streets in small groups. They would stop and visit with the kids they ran into. Over a period of time they began to attend school functions and hang out wherever the kids were. All they did was talk and listen to the kids and hang out. They became a visible masculine force in a healthy way. It didn't take long for the drugs and violence to leave their area. The idea has become popular and spread to a dozen or more cities. (www.maddads.com).

Wound #8: Contaminated God Image

Because the earthly father figure was designed by God to represent the Heavenly Father to the children of men, the young male without a father figure has a distorted image of what God is like. Since it is considered wimpy to go to church and talk about spiritual things, the young male struggles with anything to do with God. Any spirituality he may develop is contaminated by a lack of healthy fathering.

When earthly fathers become irrelevant, the Father Love of God fades from awareness in the lives of most people. The key to the generational transfer of the Christian faith is the role of the earthly father. The research demonstrates that when mothers take children to church only 28% of the children continue in the church after they leave home, but 72% continue in the church if the father participates with the children. And men are leaving the church like rats leaving a sinking ship. The average church around the world has less than 35% males in the active membership who participate on a regular basis.

The Church in America is wounded. In the United States there are more than 350,000 churches; 80% are either stagnant or decreasing in numbers. Today only 29% of the adult population can be called active, practicing Christians, while 116.85 million (41%) of the population report no religious affiliation. Thousands of pastors resign every month. Seminaries cannot turn out enough trained men and women to fill the needs for Pastoral leadership. What has happened to the American church? Men, raised by mothers or by non-involved fathers, don't find the average church relevant for their lives. They cannot picture a loving Heavenly Father because, for the most part, they have never experienced a loving involved father on earth.

Wound #9: No Role Model for Healthy Fathering

Since so many young males are raised by single Moms or weekend Dads, they have limited or no model for healthy fathering. When they get married and have children of their own, they tend to parent the way they were parented. While it is true of all people (parents tend to parent the way they were parented unless they make a definite effort to do it differently), young males without good role models are doubly handicapped.

Again, un-affirmed males often have no clear understanding of what "healthy" masculinity looks like or feels like. Masculinity is caught more that it is taught and without a father around or some surrogate father figure, the young male is in trouble.

This becomes a generational crisis because un-affirmed males cannot pass on to the next generation what they themselves do not possess. The father deprivation crisis involves more than one generation and, without a healthy injection of authentic masculinity into the equation, the crisis will only get worse.

Wound #10: Career Difficulties

Many men struggle settling into a career when they have not had a father to mentor and give them directions about their futures. Many will change jobs four or five times before they are thirty-five years of age.

For example, Phillip, an attractive 30 year old man was struggling with his career. He was intelligent, personable and appeared to have boundless energy when he was not depressed. His depression had gotten worse recently. Since college, he had changed jobs four times and he was not happy with his current position. He wanted to switch to a new area of interest...he just couldn't find anything that would hold his interest. The job hopping had caused financial troubles and his marriage was stressed to a breaking point. Phillip had never had a father's encouragement or blessing and he had no idea what he was good at. He was suffering from father deprivation wounds.

Scott was caught up in the financial crisis. His job went away. Along with the job went his self-worth and his confidence that he could find another job. The job crisis spilled over into his marriage, and when he came for counseling his life was falling apart. He had no hope or direction. His self image was frail from the severe father deprivation he suffered from childhood.

What about the Contrast?

There is a significant difference between young males raised in father deprived homes and young men raised in homes with healthy involved fathering. The evidence is over whelming. Research shows that men from healthy fathering backgrounds demonstrate the opposite characteristics from those with unhealthy fathering.

Research shows that almost all Naval and Air Force "Top Gun" pilots come from homes with a healthy father and that many top athletes, "the franchise men," also come from healthy fathering homes or they had coaches who were good surrogate fathers. Examples are Michael Jordan, Tiger Woods, Brett Favre, Emmett Smith, John Elway and the Manning boys.

A young male without a father has a significant handicap to overcome. There is a need for older men to step up and engage younger males in our culture. There are too few spiritual fathers and coaches available to help the father deprived boys of America.

CHAPTER SEVEN

Women and Father Deprivation

The impact of father deprivation affects a young girl most significantly between the ages of 3 and 10. But even in teen years, a young girl needs healthy masculine energy to balance out her psychological development.

Daughters are affected most in the stage when the opposite gender parent is the key influence. Issues from these childhood years have consequences in the adolescent years. Issues in the adolescent years are exacerbated by the effects of earlier father deprivation. While the father's delight and affection are critical from the earlier years, fathers are still vital in the adolescent years for the affirmation of the daughter's developing femininity.

The wounds that women carry from father deprivation include:

- Distrust of Men and Hostility toward Men
- Hunger for Masculine Attention and Affection
- Undifferentiated Love Feelings
- Lack of Confidence in Femininity

- Vulnerability to Addictions
- Dysfunctional Heterosexual Relationships and Marriage
- Inadequate Basis For Healthy Spirituality
- Sexual Difficulties

Wound #1: Distrust of Men and Hostility Toward Men

The first wound that is observed in women suffering from Father Deprivation is a distrust and hostility toward men. The girl raised with too little fathering often has roots of distrust and bitterness toward her father figure buried in her unconscious. *"Daddy wasn't here for me...He didn't meet my needs so what makes me think any man can or will ever really be there for me or meet my needs."*

The young girl who is not delighted in, who does not have a warm, loving affectionate relationship with her father during pre-school and elementary school years, experiences Father Deprivation. Her distrust of men and hostility toward men are easily generalized to all men in her life as she moves into adult years. The closer, more intimate the relationships in later life, the more obvious the effects. They may be very conscious of these feelings or they may be working at an unconscious level. But somewhere in her soul is that fear: *"If my father wasn't here for me, what makes me think any man will ever be here for me?"*

A young girl wants to be the delight of her father, the apple of his eye. It is a measure of her worth and value; if she does not capture her father's heart, it breaks her little girl heart. When a girl fails to win her father's attention and affection, she begins to feel deep seated resentment. Before too long, the resentment becomes anger and rage. It may be a passive aggressiveness, but it is still the strongest emotion she has toward her father. As she gets older, the anger grows and by the teen years it may blossom into full blown rebellion. She ignores her father like he ignored her. She turns her attention to other men almost to spite her father.

At this early age the girl is trying to capture Dad's heart. It is a testing time for the young girl's sense of self worth and value. If she feels she flunked this period of testing, she never manages to develop a sense of deep trust with her father or any other man.

This distrust and hostility is manifested in the girl's adult heterosexual relationships. While the feelings of distrust and hostility may be unconscious, these affect the woman's ability to draw close to any male with whom she seeks to have an intimate relationship. The deeper the commitment, the more these feelings appear to manifest, and they often feed marital transferences. Many women are unaware how their early childhood anger and distrust at their father feeds their distrust and anger even after they have been married for twenty years or longer.

Traumatic experiences, such as childhood physical or sexual abuse in her relationship with her father or other men, add exponentially to this distrust and hostility. A painful story was told to me in counseling about a young girl, a beautiful blonde four year old, jumping on her parent's bed. Her father comes into the room and urges the girl to jump to him. The girl is coaxed into jumping. As she flies through the air, her father moves. She hits the dresser hard and lands on the floor. While she is lying on the floor crying in pain, her father stands over her and says, *"That will teach you never to trust anyone."* Such betrayals wound a child's ability to trust anyone ever. It was no wonder that the young woman who told me this story had never been able to have a successful loving relationship with the opposite sex.

When a woman, who experienced abuse in childhood, has emotional or verbal abuse in her adult life, it often exacerbates her reaction and distrust. Even a Christian woman who has forgiven the original abuser can still have unfinished emotional wounds that make it extremely difficult for her to trust as an adult. Forgiveness is the appropriate Christian response, but forgiveness alone does not heal the wound, and it certainly does not heal the women's ability to trust.

Wound #2: Hunger for Masculine Attention and Affection

This hunger for masculine affection and attention is probably the most powerful driving wound of Father Deprivation in a woman's life. This wound is the result of the lack of a warm, affectionate relationship with her father during the opposite gender stage. It may leave a woman with an almost unquenchable desire to be held and to receive affection from a male. While this need is disguised in numerous ways, it underlies much of the conflicts in her dating and marriage relationships.

A young girl, denied affection and attention, hungry for her Daddy to hold her, cuddle her, lovingly touch her, carries a painful problem into her adult relationships. Often, in an attempt to meet her affection/attention hunger, a woman will involve herself sexually, give her body sexually just to feel a man's arms around her. She accepts genital contact to get her affection and attention needs met. These needs increase her sexual vulnerability from early in life. In time she comes to resent the very men she uses to meet her affection needs because they use her sexually and leave her.

A research study in Vancouver, Canada dealing with young teens, male and female who had turned to prostitution, found that these teens turned to prostitution to satisfy their need for affection and attention. They reported that this drive for affection was the primary reason given by the majority of these young prostitutes. Too often we do not understand how strong the drive for affection is in children deprived of the loving touch of a parent.

Susan was in her mid-thirties, but she looked sixteen. She told the story of her first sexual experience. When she was twelve years old, an older teenage boy seduced her. She said she had never had any male pay her attention or show her affection. When they had sex, she said, *"It felt like my heart passed through my organs into his heart."* For the first time in her life, she felt a man's delight and pleasure in her. She had never known her father's affection or delight.

Kay had worked as a flight attendant for a major airline for years. She had been sexually involved with many men over the years; enticing them, enjoying them and quickly dropping each one. In

counseling she freely discussed that it was the affection and closeness before and after intercourse that was most meaningful to her.
She admitted that she "endured" sex for the warmth and touching
that came with it. Over the years, her pattern of loving and leaving
began to concern her. She had sought counseling to gain some
personal understanding and healing. What she discovered was the
impact the distant and non-affectionate relationship with her father
had on her when she was younger.

Marlene was twenty-five years old. Her husband caught her
having an affair and demanded she go into counseling. In the first
session I asked Marlene if this was the first affair she had. She
laughed and said, *"No, I have had so many men over the past three
years I have lost count."* She estimated over three hundred men in
three years.

I asked Marlene if that was because she liked sex so much. She
said *"No, I have never even had an orgasm."* What she revealed, as
we worked in counseling, was the pattern of a non-involved, non-
affectionate father when she was young. Then in her young teen
years an older boy connected with her. She quickly learned that she
could get her affection and attention needs met by *"letting the boys
have what they wanted."*

Researchers have found that the father's influence on the
daughter begins earlier than had been thought and indicates that the
daughter's experiences with the father from early infancy are related
to the daughter's ability to trust other males. William Appleton, in
his excellent book, Fathers and Daughters, states:

> *"Women deprived of father's love and attention in childhood,
> have underdeveloped self-esteem and find it hard to believe a
> man could totally love and accept them."*

If the daughter's first experience of loving across gender lines
is missing...Daddy was not there...a girl can grow into a young
woman who needs adulation from men but has difficulty ever really
loving them. Researchers and psychologists would say that what is
missing in these women is any real experience of affection toward
and from their fathers. A small girl and the woman she later becomes

lacks some basic understanding of the opposite sex if she has not had a loving father to play with and cope with...to get angry at, to be admired by and to love and admire in return. Daddy is meant to be a daughter's first love.

Famous Illustrations:

When this area of need is not met in the young girl's life, she may be vulnerable to older males in her teen and young adult years. Many girls have given their bodies visually (movies, pornography, etc.) and sexually to get their affection and attention needs met.

Many famous female movie stars have obvious father deprivation. Sophia Loren is a good case study. Sophia's father had seduced her mother but abandoned her and her daughter at birth, leaving them to face life in a small Italian village shamed and alone. Sophia met her father the first time when she was five years old. He gave her a small blue little race car with her name on it and even today she will tell you that it is the best gift she ever received. Sophia writes in her autobiography about her Daddy: *"I sought him everywhere. I married him. I made my best films with him. I curried his favor. I sat on his lap and snuggled him...I saw him only a few times...yet he dominated my life."*

In a Parade Magazine article, a question was asked about Audrey Hepburn. The question concerned why she always worked with older guys like Humphrey Bogart, Gary Cooper, Fred Astaire and Cary Grant. The magazine response was enlightening: *"Hepburn spent 24 years looking for her father, who abandoned the family when she was six...After they were reunited, Hepburn took care of her Dad until he died...In our opinion, that search for a father figure influenced her choice of roles opposite much older men."*

Marilyn Monroe's life and many other beautiful young women in Hollywood could be used to demonstrate the hunger for male affection and attention so many of them suffer from. The well publicized events in the lives of so many of Hollywood's young "Pop Tarts", as they have been labeled in the media, likely result from the same kind of father deprivation issues. Perhaps much of the beauty and fashion industry is driven by the desire to compensate for a lost father's attention through male attraction and seduction.

The best research available concerning father-absence reveals that daughters of divorcees tended to be aggressive and forward with males. They sought attention from men and tried to be near them and have physical contact with male peers. Father deprived and father absent daughters are more precocious in their dating behavior.

The young girl who is deprived of her father's attentions in her early years will try to get as much attention as she can from grandfather, uncles and cousins. As a teenager, there is a chance that she will be "boy crazy". Later she may become highly skilled at seduction and provoking the masculine attention she craves, but not know what to do with it once she is in a long term commitment like marriage.

The great needs emotionally a young girl has during this stage of development are for affection and attention from the opposite sex parent. She wants to know that she is special and that her father delights in her. She wants to dance for him and be celebrated by him.

Many of the conflicts in marriage and other adult heterosexual relationships can be better understood if seen in the light of an unsatisfied hunger for masculine attention and affection. Adult struggles often are symbolic re-enactments of childhood, with the woman either working to satisfy her emotional needs or reacting to the scars left from her hurts.

Wound #3: Undifferentiated Love Feelings

Children are not born knowing how to love. They are born with certain needs and, as their mother and father meet these needs, the child learns what feels like love. This feeling of being loved develops through four levels.

The first feeling that feels like love is the way a child feels when his or her physical needs are met. This love feeling is the first love feeling that develops in the first year of life.

The second love feeling is the way it feels when a child gets his or her way. When parents allow the child to feed himself or choose what he wants to wear or eat, etc. he feels loved. This love feeling begins to develop around 18 months of age through the preschool years.

The third way of feeling loved is the feeling a child has when he or she gets the undivided attention of other people. Having attention focused on them feels like they are important and loved. This way of feeling loved usually develops from about age four or five into later grade school years.

Once a person learns to feel loved at any of these stages, similar life experiences (having physical needs met, getting his/her own way, and having undivided attention) will always feel loving.

The most mature way of feeling loved is the fourth level of feeling loved. It is the feeling a person has when his act of love is responded to by another person. This develops later in life and some people may never move to this level, remaining stuck in one or more of the three earlier stages.

These four levels of feeling loved are all about non-erotic love feelings. Every child is born with undifferentiated love feelings, meaning they do not normally have any sense of erotic love feelings in these early stages. The potential for erotic feelings is there, in that the body parts that feel good in adults feel good for the child, but they do not have the maturity to understand about erotic love feelings as adults do.

Healthy parents give their child healthy non-erotic love and affection, and the child returns the love feelings to the parents. The child's love feelings are undifferentiated and so the child gives all their love feelings, both the potential erotic and non-erotic to the parents. The parents return appropriate non-erotic feelings and children begin to make a differentiation in their inner soul. The parent of the opposite gender is most critical to the child at this time in their development. For the girl this is the father figure and it is critical that he return only non-erotic love feelings to his daughter.

When a young girl does not receive affection and non-erotic love from her father, or if she is sexualized at an early age, she will not make a differentiation in her own inner person between the erotic and non-erotic love feelings. She grows up with undifferentiated love feelings.

If a girl has made the differentiation in her inner person, then when she begins to become aware of the opposite sex in her teens, she can lead with non-erotic love feelings. If she has not made this differentiation between her erotic and non-erotic love feelings, she will offer all her love feelings, erotic and non-erotic, to her dates, and they will typically return erotic love feelings. Some women, as well as some men, never learn to differentiate their love feelings so they tend to interpret all affection from the opposite sex with erotic overtones.

Wound #4: Lack of Confidence in Femininity

When a young girl does not have the delight of her father in her early years, it leaves her with a wounded self-worth. She wonders if she is feminine enough to ever win a man's heart if she couldn't win her Dad's heart.

When she moves into puberty and her feminine body begins to develop, she begins to model her femininity after her mother. But, even as she is learning how to become a woman, she still has one eye on her father. In her heart she is wondering if Daddy notices her development, if he approves and thinks she is getting to be beautiful. She wants to hear and needs to hear her father say something like: *"Honey you are so beautiful! I better get a big stick to beat all the men away from our front porch."* The non-erotic affirmation of the adolescent girl is critical for her to have confidence in her femininity.

> *"A father's inability to connect with his daughter causes her feelings of rejection, abandonment, self-doubt, anxiety, fear and sadness...Teenage daughters need to be emotionally supported and refueled by their fathers, since men's opinions are so central to them. Accepting the many changes associated with adolescence, particularly sexuality, is not just an internal process. Girls rely on others, especially their fathers, to help them integrate sexual maturity into their personal identities and lifestyles."*
>
> Margo Maine, <u>Father-Hunger</u>

Wound #5: Vulnerability to Addictions

The emotional pain that a girl feels over the deprivation of her father's affection and attention is hidden deep inside her heart and soul. She experiences shame and regret over feeling that she is not pretty enough or special enough for Daddy. This can often result in the adolescent girl trying to get male affection and attention and can drive her toward different forms of addictive behaviors. If the girl was sexualized by sexual abuse in her childhood, the more pain she feels. The greater the quantity of pain she carries in her soul, the more likely she will move into addictions.

Many times there is guilt and shame about inappropriate choices the girl made to try to get her needs met. She was vulnerable to certain temptations sexually and relationally and now she is living with the pain of her choices. Alcohol and drugs and other addictive behaviors become the way to deaden this pain.

Wound #6: Dysfunctional Heterosexual Relationships and Marriage

This particular wound has to do with the consequences of some of the other wounds and the lack of healthy modeling. Since the young girl did not experience a healthy family life growing up, it is likely that she does not have a good model of what a healthy relationship with men or marriage should be like. These women often have marital and sexual problems that they don't understand and can't explain. Many of these women end up divorced.

> *"Deprived though she may have been of a father, many a woman will seek out serial romances or marriages for the thrill of conquest. Daddy may have turned her down, but other men will not. She needs the excitement of a new face, a new body, a new presence. However, enduring relationships are not her strong suit."*
>
> Sonja Friedman, <u>Men Are Just Desserts</u>

The problem of marital transference presents itself in the counseling office many times. It is a problem of relating emotionally to a husband as if he were her Daddy. In every marriage there are some emotions and feelings that get transferred to a person's mate that originally developed in the relationship with the person's opposite sex parent. In marriages when the wife comes from a home background with an ineffective father, she relates to her husband emotionally as if he were her Daddy, seeking to have her husband meet the emotional needs that were not met by her father.

This transference of emotions can be particularly damaging in the area of sexual intimacy in marriage. (This wound in men was addressed in Chapter Five under Sexual Difficulties.) In counseling, a number of women suffering from frigidity or low sex drives said that their emotions during sexual activities were almost repulsive, similar to what they thought they might feel if their father approached them sexually. One woman even said that having sex with her husband was what she imagined it would be like to have sex with her father.

Not having their needs met for non-erotic affection from their fathers, unconsciously they are responding to their mate's physical affection as they would to their father's affection as a little girl. These women displace their paternal distrust and hostility to their husbands, which makes it difficult for them to respond sexually. These women often have trouble distinguishing between erotic and non-erotic affection of any kind from members of the opposite sex.

Wound #7: Inadequate Basis for Healthy Spirituality

When a young girl does not have a healthy loving relationship with her father, it impacts her image of God. She tends to picture God being like her Daddy, for good or bad. The distrust and hostility toward her Dad get transferred to her Higher Power. She often has authority issues that also contaminate her spirituality.

Research demonstrates that the father's attitudes about religion and spirituality have a greater impact on the daughter than does the mother's. The father is the parent that communicates what is important and what is not important in many key areas of life.

Wound #8: Sexual Difficulties

A daughter's first love is supposed to be her Daddy. The young girl who feels loved and delighted in by her father when she is in the second stage (between the ages of 3 and 8-9) will be better prepared to have healthy heterosexual relationships later in life. When she has not received the love and affection she desired, then she is much more likely to engage in promiscuous behavior and at an earlier age.

Research also shows that girls who have unmet father needs also have more difficulty enjoying sex in their married lives than girls who were delighted in and who received lots of father's affection and attention. The girl who felt safe and special in her father's arms when she was young will have little difficulty relating sexually to her husband in marriage.

> *"A central theme emerging from the low-orgasmic women was that they lacked meaningful relationships with their fathers. Low-orgasmic women described uninvolved fathers who did not have well defined expectations or rules for their daughters. They also recalled much physical and psychological father-absence during early childhood. In contrast, high orgasmic women were more likely to perceive their fathers as having had definite and demanding expectations and a concern for their enforcement. Findings revealed that the father is much more important than the mother in the development of orgasmic adequacy in females."*
>
> Michael E. Lamb, <u>The Role of the Father in Child Development</u>

Every man in a woman's life is a link in the chain that begins with Daddy. Girls raised with Father Deprivation and Father Absence suffer many soul wounds and have many vulnerabilities. The impact of these wounds not only affects the woman; it impacts the way she responds to her husband and even her sons. If she divorces, she carries her unfinished issues to the next relationship, and her sons often become targets of her unresolved anger toward their father.

The research does not lie; your personal knowledge of your life, your friend's lives and of the culture we all live in does not lie. Father Deprivation causes a major wound for daughters as well as sons. You, your children and your grandchildren all deserve healthy fathering.

If nothing changes, nothing changes. And your children and grandchildren will be victims of the same kind of wounds from father deprivation. Now is the time to make a change. Our daughters and sons deserve it! So do our grandchildren.

CHAPTER EIGHT

Father Wounds and Homosexuality

There are many people in our culture who have determined that they have a homosexual orientation. They are not immune to father wounds. In fact many of these individuals have an awareness of their father wounds, but have not found healing for their pain.

Homosexual Men

Gay men can have a significant wound of Father Deprivation. They were often raised in a home with a father who was absent, abusive or just simply emotionally unavailable. The father might wound the young male before the ages of four or five by abuse, severe criticism or rejection. The father, out of his own wounded-ness, strikes out and verbally or even physically wounds the young child. This results in the child never feeling any emotional empathy or identification to the father figure. The child, from very early child-hood, feels unsafe with his father figure.

When the identification with the father is broken by abuse or neglect, an over identification with the mother often occurs. The child seeks mother attention and empathizes with her against the father and identifies himself with her femininity.

However, as the boy develops and prepares to move through puberty, he begins to pull away from Mother, but has no father figure he trusts to draw him toward masculinity. He comes to resent mother's power and control. He may even identify with her power rather than rebel against the feminine.

Yet in his personality, there is a hunger for the masculine and a need to find a connection with the masculine world. It is this hunger for masculine affection and attention that often makes the young male vulnerable to his first homosexual liaison. In essence this young hunger for masculine affirmation is sexualized and he finds some fulfillment in masculine love.

He was a big handsome 28 year old man. As he shared his story, he began to cry. He was certainly not happy in his own skin. He told about his father's death when he was about four years of age. His mother never remarried. He wept and said, *"I never felt a man's delight until the first time I had sex with one."* His hunger for masculine affection and approval was sexualized.

Another young man walked in on his older cousins masturbating in a group. He said he was going to tell on them but instead they enticed him to participate with them. He did and found masculine approval. This experience embarked him on a homosexual journey.

Homosexual Women

The father wound for lesbian women has to do with abuse and distance from the father. Often the abuse is from a male authority figure, and it may be physical, sexual, verbal or emotional. Some male abuses the young girl, her mother or siblings, resulting in the young girl having an extreme distrust and fear of any males to whom she might be vulnerable. This wound can often combine with the wound of having a mother who is unable to offer much warmth and affection for the young girl.

As she moves into puberty, the usual attraction to males is a fearful issue for the girl, so she often turns away from her own femininity to avoid being attractive to males. Her hunger for feminine affection and attention, not being fulfilled by a healthy mother daughter relationship, makes her vulnerable to her first lesbian encounter.

Jane was a college grad working with other girls on a college campus. She found herself attracted to the girls she worked with. Her father deprivation wounds made her feel safer with the girls than she did with the men she met. This led to her being seduced by an older lesbian, yet she did not find the comfort she hungered for. After struggling with her feelings for several months, she sought help through counseling. She found a male counselor and, in finding a safe place with him, was able to understand how her father deprivation wound had led her into certain homosexual behaviors. She determined that she was not a lesbian and eventually married an individual of the opposite sex and had a family.

What about Homophobia?

Homophobia is the label given to people who have a fear of being associated with homosexuals or who have anger or other negative emotions about such associations. For some people, this is a real fear. For others, it is not the homosexual aspect; rather it is the fear of being close to anyone.

Some men and women have a fear of being close to homosexuals because they might recognize some attraction to the affection and attention they desire from those individuals. This may well be an expression in males of the hunger for masculine affection and attention they did not receive in their childhoods. For some women, it could reflect a hunger for the affection and attention they did not receive from their mothers.

If homophobia is related to a father wound, then it can be faced as any other father wound (addressed in the final chapter). If there is no father wound involved, then talking about your fears with a counselor can usually help you alleviate them.

Consequences in a person's life are determined by the severity of the wounds and the way that person responds to the wounding. Because each person is unique and each response is individual, the behaviors that result are unique. But the wounds are very real. Whether the person determines he or she is homosexual or heterosexual, individuals still need to seek healing for their woundedness.

CHAPTER NINE

Healing Father Wounds

M any people in our culture suffer wounds from their father: abuse wounds and/or deprivation wounds. Some of these individuals do not realize that father issues are the reasons they are in pain; others know too well that their pain is the result of father wounds.

Wounds from a parent are insidious, difficult at times to recognize and painful to overcome. Father wounds are felt in many ways, usually contaminating other areas of our life. Father Abuse and Father Absent wounds seem to be easier to discern; Father Deprivation wounds can take on more disguises.

Since for most people, their biological father was the first male to imprint their lives, they assume that everyone had a father like theirs. So whatever difficulty they had, they make the assumption that everyone has the same issues about Daddy. *"He is the only father I had. I didn't know anything different."*

But there are many stories, so much pain.

A 40 year old woman, who had danced as an exotic dancer for nearly twenty years, broke down and cried because she still could not feel that she was special to her Dad who deserted the family when she was five years old.

A 35 year old woman, who deserted her husband and children, could not trust any man because of her experiences in her teen years with a stepfather who kept making sexual advances towards her.

A young man, who couldn't hold down a job, kept hearing his father's words; *"You are just stupid! You will never amount to anything."*

A man, nearly sixty years old, was paralyzed with fear of intimacy because he remembered the ugliness between his mother and his father.

A pilot for a major airline broke down and wept great tears of shame remembering the different men his mother had in the house after his father left.

A business executive described how his alcoholic father used to chase his mother and brother out of the house. He told how his father almost pulled his arm off when he grabbed him as he was going out the window trying to escape his father's violence.

In men's groups, guys often talk about and grieve over the fathers they never had. They will talk about the last time they saw their Dads alive or the last thing they remembered hearing their fathers say.

The stories could go on and on. There are many wounded people. So many broken hearts. So many relationships that are contaminated by these unhealed wounds. Father wounds contaminate all of our relationships and, the more intimate the relationships, the greater the complications and contamination.

The term "wound" implies that I received something I did not ask for and probably would not have chosen if I had a choice. Someone else administered whatever caused my wound. It is the result of living in an imperfect world, and I respond to the wound from my immature self. Because we live in this imperfect world and everyone we meet is a resident of this same planet, it is inevitable that we all will be wounded and that we will all respond in our own ways to our wounds. Our parents, as the primary care givers in the early years of our lives, are also residents of this same world. Like all the rest of us, they dealt with us and with their lives out of their own wounded lives. They did the best they could with what they knew. Since no one has ever had perfect parents, all of us, in some way, are wounded in our relationships with them.

The Healing Process

There are depths within all of us that we do not comprehend. God has so structured us as human beings and our abilities have been so damaged by living in a fallen world that we are unable to plumb these depths by ourselves.

We all suffer soul and heart wounds in this imperfect fallen world. God has equipped us with brains that sometimes enable us to sweep memories into a dark closet called the unconscious, where we hope and pray they will simply fade away. But it never happens because these memories we have swept into the dark closet are loaded with emotions and feelings. The facts of the events may be out of our awareness, but the emotions and feelings are very much alive and attached to other life experiences. If we repress and bury these toxic emotions and feelings, the time will surely come when these buried feelings will suddenly burst uncontrolled into our lives. It is better to deal with these emotions instead of burying them.

The Two Ages of Your Life

Every human being lives at two different age levels. First there is our chronological age. I am sixty-seven years old. I cannot be forty-seven. Chronological age progresses, no matter what our life experiences may be, until the day we die. Chronological age is a result of the aging process we all experience.

We also have an emotional age...the age we feel and the age at which we live emotionally. We all know people who "don't act their age." And we all have had life experiences when we reacted as if we were much younger emotionally and behaviorally. Perhaps you were in a movie and something in the film triggered your tears and you began to cry like a young child. This was my experience. I took my kids years ago to see the Disney Classic "Song of the South" and suddenly found myself crying like a broken hearted young boy. Not just tears streaming down my face, but deep gut wrenching sobs. I was so embarrassed that I had to leave the movie. I was thirty-eight years old chronologically, but I felt seven or eight years old at that moment. I emotionally was a young boy again. The scene that impacted me so was one in which the little boy runs crying after his daddy.

When we have life experiences that wound our souls and we are unable to release the tears and the pain, we repress this emotional energy. We sweep it into the dark closet of our unconscious memory and, unwittingly, we block to some degree our emotional growth at that age. These memories are very much alive and loaded with emotions and feelings. The facts of the events may be out of our awareness, but the emotions and feelings are very much alive and contaminate our relationships and experiences. These emotions and feelings reside in some deep place in our souls, just waiting for the right trigger event to release the pain, fear or anger. When that event happens, you will feel that younger age with the emotions of the painful event all over again.

Scars on Our Souls

Remember the human personality is formed, deformed and transformed in relationships. You are who you are today because of the way your inner person was shaped by the relationships and life experiences (good and bad) you have had.

These wounds are to our soul, our inner person, and are not visible to the casual observer. But the marks are there deep in our souls. David Seamands uses a great analogy in his book, Healing For Damaged Emotions:

> *"If you visit the far West, you will see those beautiful giant sequoia and redwood trees. In most of the parks the natural-ists can show you a cross section of a giant tree they have*

*cut, and point out that the rings of the tree reveal the devel-
opmental history, year by year. Here is a ring that represents
a year when there was a terrible drought. Here are a couple
of rings from years when there was too much rain. Here's
where the tree was struck by lightening. Here are some
normal years of growth. This ring shows a forest fire that
almost destroyed the tree. Here's another of savage blight
and disease. All of this lies embedded in the heart of the tree,
representing the autobiography of its growth."*

Seamands adds:

*"Just a few minutes beneath the protective bark, the
concealing, protective mask, are the recorded rings of our
lives."*

So it is with our lives and our life experiences with our fathers.
We carry in our souls the rings that testify of our wounds and pain.
If your father was absent and never there, you carry wounds about
the lack of fathering you experienced. If your father was present
and abusive, you have other wounds. If your father was there physically, but not emotionally connected with you, you have another
kind of wound. It is doubtful that any person reaching maturity can
do so without some soul wounds from their family of origin. All of
our families were dysfunctional to some degree because all of our
parents were wounded. We all have wounds that make us vulnerable
in this imperfect world.

Another quote from Seamands:

*"In the rings of our thoughts and emotions, the record is
there; the memories are recorded, and all alive. And they
directly and deeply affect our concepts, our feelings, our
relationships. They affect the way we look at life, at God, at
others and ourselves."*

Father wounds can be healed through a process that involves
dealing with your intellectual understanding, your emotional experi-

ences, your habits and behaviors as well as your spiritual life. This healing is usually a transformational healing process and involves many life experiences peeled off one layer at a time. You have to intentionally choose to work the program and face the pain in this healing process. It is an intentional activity.

As we participate in the healing process, the truth moves from head knowledge into heart knowledge and begins to release the emotional chains that have controlled the way we live. Our internal character and nature are changed through the transformational process and, consequently, our external behaviors change to reflect this same transformation.

Why Look at Our Past?

Some people question why we need to revisit our past, look at our history. Some believe that our history is not important; others believe it is a shifting of blame to our parents. Some reason that if I cannot remember the facts of my childhood then I have forgotten the life experiences and they have no impact on my adult life. Some people even question the existence of the unconscious mind. The prophet Jeremiah wrote:

"The heart is deceitful above all things and beyond cure. Who can understand it?" (Jeremiah 17:9)

And the person our sinful fallen heart deceives the most is our self.

If our history does not matter, then how we live our lives every day does not matter. Nothing from the past could impact our lives; literally there would be no learning from our life experiences. If history and life experiences do not matter, then it does not matter how we raise our children because they won't remember anyway. So I could treat a child anyway I wanted to and it wouldn't matter because the child would never remember what has happened. Healthy people know this is not true but it is the false reasoning of many child abusers and pedophiles.

Every experience of our lives is stored in the marvelous memory that God built into us. Every thought, every experience and every feeling that we have ever experienced is stored in the memory system of our brain and our body. These memories do matter and our history is important.

We look at our past because our life experiences are important. Nowhere in the Scriptures did God ever tell His people to forget their history. Instead, He told His people to remember their life experiences and to enshrine them with feasts and celebrations. He told them to collect stones and mark different locations with monuments so that when their children would see the monument, the fathers could re-tell the story of God's deliverances.

God uses our past history as a teaching tool for intergenerational transfer of the faith (Joshua 4:19-24).

God uses our history, our testimonies of what He has done, to overcome the "evil one" (Revelation 12:10-11).

God uses history to remind us to not fall into the same sins as the nation Israel did (I Corinthians 10:6, 11).

We are the product of our history. We became who we are through all of the things we have experienced. If my memory and history about painful life experiences do not matter, then neither do my memories and history of the happy, fun, loving events matter.

Our personal history and life experiences do matter. Remember it was God who designed the human mind with the marvelous memory system!

The Prophet Isaiah (Isaiah 43:18-19) and the Apostle Paul (Philippians 3:7-14) tell the readers to "forget" things from the past in the sense of "let go" of your history, whether it is a negative history (Isaiah speaking of the nation Israel) or positive history (Paul speaking of his credentials vv.7-8). The implication is that God can change our history and He desires us to draw our worth and value from Him and not from our past, whether it is good or bad. We are not to allow our history to define us, name us or control us.

We should look at our personal life history the way a medical doctor looks at our medical history: it is a teaching tool to enable us to be more effective in our present situation. When you go to the emergency room with a bad stomach ache, the doctor does not immediately throw you on the operating table and cut out your appendix. If he does not do a medical history first, he might be surprised to find that your appendix was removed twenty years ago. So the doctor looks at your medical history to gain understanding that can be applied to the current medical problem. We should do the same with our personal life history.

We are to learn from our history, not be controlled by it. When we blame someone else for our problems or wounds, we have removed ourselves from the place where God can give us healing. We have given away the very things that God wanted to use to transform us. Nothing can be healed until it becomes real and we take ownership and responsibility for our situation.

So we look at our history to understand, not to blame. It doesn't matter who pushed you in the mud hole, you have to get yourself out.

Our personal history is important because God wants us to learn from it and because it is stored in our mind and is a part of our soul. So we look at our history to understand, not to shift the blame. A better understanding often leads to quicker healing and a more effective growth process.

Understanding Soul Wounds

"Every man carries a wound. I have never met a man without one...And every wound whether it's assaultive or passive, delivers with it a message."

John Eldredge, <u>Wild At Heart</u>

Wounds are common to all men and women. Some wounds are deep inside hidden from the casual observer, others are obvious to every one the person meets. These wounds changed our perspective and changed our lives.

All father wounds are soul wounds. There is an analogy that can help us understand what happens when we suffer a soul wound such as a father wound. For this analogy, picture a cut on your hand, a gash across the palm. It is a deep cut, so you wash it off and put a bandage around it. You have hidden it from your sight, swept it into the closet. Now for a day or so, you might not worry about the wound, but then on the third or four day, it begins to hurt again. It is still bandaged and wrapped, so you assume nothing is wrong. But after another day or so, the wound begins to drain and has an awful odor and your whole hand begins to swell. When you get to the doctor's office you discover that you now have a very serious blood infection. Your wound was contaminated by germs that infected the wound.

A similar thing happens with father and soul wounds from our past that we sweep into the dark closet. These soul and father wounds get infected and contaminated, not by germs, but by the lies of the evil one. Satan plants his lies into our lives through soul wounds. We sweep the wounds into the dark closet and try to forget that they ever happened. Some of the most insidious soul wounds are wounds from your experiences with your father. The wound of an orphan heart is the result of the lies Satan attaches to it.

The latest brain research is clarifying how these lies impact our lives.

Brain Research and Wounds

The most recent brain research has discovered that the brain does not store memories like a computer does. The brain is morphed by every experience we have...we become what we experience. The brain does not mechanically store the facts and life experiences that it acquires, it is changed by these very experiences. Each time a person interacts with the world around them, the brain changes to engulf the new information. The brain is even more marvelous than we ever imagined.

Dr. Caroline Leaf is a Christian researcher who works to help people discover their potential by changing the way they think. In her book, <u>Who Switched Off My Brain?</u>, she says that every thought has a corresponding electrochemical reaction in our brain. When we think, chemicals course through our brains and our bodies in a complex, electrochemical feedback loop. These chemicals carry to every cell of our bodies the same messages that are in our brains. She says the mind and body are integrally connected and writes:

"In effect, these networks create 'copies' of your 'thought life' along with the emotions that the chemicals coursing through your blood stream literally carry around your whole body like an information highway. Information molecules are then able to cause changes at the cellular level, actually restructuring the cell's makeup on the outside and the DNA on the inside."

Dr. Leaf goes on to say that abuse experiences release negative chemicals that travel through our bodies changing the basic cell structure of our bodies. She also gives us the good news that positive thoughts release good chemicals that cause our brains to flourish and enable us to have mental and physical health.

This is wonderful news for everyone who has father wounds. This means that God can totally reprogram our mind and our bodies through what we think about and fill our minds with. God can heal our souls so we can find complete freedom from the pain and shame of the abuse. He has already created the structures and processes within us that the Holy Spirit can work through to accomplish our healing.

The Inner Healing Process

Inner healing is a process through which the grace and mercy of God is applied by the Holy Spirit to the deep soul wounds of an individual. This process has been called by many names down through the years: healing of memories, soul healing, inner healing and transformational healing. Agnes Sanford coined the phrase "healing of memories" in the 1940's and 50's. John Wimber, the founder of the Vineyard Church movement, was a man greatly used of God to bring healing to thousands of people. He defined inner healing as a process in which the Holy Spirit brings forgiveness of sins and emotional renewal to people suffering from damaged minds, wills, and emotions. David Seamands defined inner healing as ministering to and praying for damaged emotions and unhealed memories. Healing the soul wounds from a person's experiences with his/her father certainly fits within these definitions.

We begin with the realization that God is the One who does the healing (Exodus 15:26; Psalm 103:3; Isaiah 53:5; I Peter 2:24). God is the healer. All healing, no matter how it comes, is from God. He created the human body and mind to be self-healing organisms and He implemented in His creation systems that make healing possible. He also uses His Word (written and spoken) as well as His people as tools in the healing process.

Sometimes emotional and spiritual healing begins with a "power encounter" with God's Spirit, a crisis event or a major spiritual encounter with the power of God. Such an event may happen at a healing conference, in a prayer encounter, in church or when you are alone with God in the mountains or on the lake. God can meet you anywhere at any time. We should live with an expectant anticipation that our loving Father is going to show up...maybe in the next moment (even as you are reading this page) or tonight or tomorrow. We cannot structure such healing encounters; these are special gifts that God gives through His love and mercy.

For most Christians, emotional and spiritual healing is a transformational healing process. The process may include numerous "power encounters" with the Spirit of God over several months or years, but true healing and transformation is a life long process as each person intentionally seeks to become like Christ.

"Now the Lord is the Spirit, and where the Spirit of the Lord is, there is freedom. And we, who with unveiled faces all reflect the Lord's glory, are being transformed into His like-

*ness with ever-increasing glory which comes from the Lord,
who is the Spirit."*

II Corinthians 3:17-18

In the next chapter we will look at the specific steps in the healing
process.

CHAPTER TEN

The Steps for Healing

The inner healing involved in healing father wounds is a process through which the grace and mercy of God are applied by the Holy Spirit to your deep soul wounds. Many people in our culture suffer soul wounds from their father's abuse (aggressive wounds) and deprivation (passive wounds). These wounds impact our lives and contaminate all of our relationships.

Father wounds can be healed. Healing involves intellectual understanding, emotional healing and spiritual transformation. The Holy Spirit, working in your soul, makes real in you all that Jesus did for you. The healing is a transformational process and involves facing many life experiences, allowing the Holy Spirit to peel these off one layer at a time. You have to intentionally choose to work the program and to face the pain in this healing process.

Jesus Christ, through the Holy Spirit, is the agent of transformational healing. He is the Great Healer in the New Testament and in the world today. The Spirit of God uses two tools for our healing:

(1) The Word of God, both written and spoken.

(2) The people of God.

We read about God's love, mercy and grace and these realities touch us deeply as the Holy Spirit implants these truths in our minds. Then, as we participate in new family relationships within the Body of Christ, the Spirit transforms this head knowledge into heart knowledge and begins to release the emotional chains that have impacted the way we behave. Our internal character and nature are changed through the transformational process so that we are unconsciously different in all of our relationships.

For most of us, when God wants us to really understand His nature, His love and unconditional acceptance, He wraps these truths in human flesh so we can experience these and feel these truths at the human level. His people make His love believable and feel-able.

So how do we apply what we learned in the previous chapter to healing our Father wounds?

STEP # 1: Ask God to reveal to you what He wants to heal.

Ask God, through His Holy Spirit, to search out your wounds and vulnerabilities and enable you to feel the pain of these wounds. Pray and ask God to show you what He wants to heal. The following paraphrase of Psalm 139:23-24 is a great prayer and makes a good place to begin:

> *"Search me, O God, and know my heart.*
> *Investigate me and know my anxious thoughts.*
> *See if there is any way of pain in me,*
> *and lead me in Your ways,*
> *of healing and understanding."*

Father wounds are real; they impact your life and your relationships. As God enables you to see and recognize your wounds, accept them as real and recognize how these wounds impact your life and all of your relationships.

Nothing can be healed until it becomes real to you in your own feelings. This step involves making the wounds conscious, owning and accepting the reality of your own personal experiences with your father. This includes gaining insight and understanding at the intellectual level and also at the emotional level, letting yourself feel your pain.

Own these life experiences as what you really experienced. It is only when these become real to you that they can be healed. This step involves making the wounds conscious, owning and accepting the reality of your own personal experiences with your father.

It is often helpful to write out painful memories so you can accurately deal with them. In order to access these memories, you may need to explore your relationship with your father (or lack thereof) with a friend, pastor or counselor and then write out the feelings that you experience as you talk about your father.

What is the best memory you have of your father? What is the worst memory? Do you remember his laugh, his smile, his smell? Did anything you read in this book stir up your feelings? Write about what you feel, not just the facts of those memories. This is the process of externalizing (bringing into the light) your memories and feelings so they can be healed.

STEP #2: Accept the reality that your wounds have been contaminated emotionally and spiritually by Satan and his lies.

Every emotional wound becomes an attachment point for the enemy and an entry point for the enemy and his propaganda. The enemy's power is in the lies that he implants through our wounds.

Every wound becomes an attachment point for lies. These lies may come from an idle comment or from your imagination, but these lies carry emotional pain and increase its power in your life. These lies are implanted in your wounds. It is these lies that cause a person to develop an orphan's heart.

Begin this step of healing by prayerfully asking God to reveal to you the lies you have believed about yourself, about your father and others. Also ask Him to reveal the lies you have believed about God. Let the Spirit reveal to you what all these lies are.

As you journal these wound descriptions, write about the lies that you become aware of that are attached to your wounds. Ask your counselor or some friends to talk with you about these lies and how to break away from their power and the consequences that linger from your experiences with your father.

For example, the young girl who suffers from father deprivation thinks something must be wrong with her because her father did not pay attention to her. Another example would be the child who believes that his bad behavior caused his father to leave and divorce his mother. Children who have been sexually abused believe they were the cause of the abuse, that they are bad and broken beyond repair. These lies are explanations that the human mind creates to help victims rationalize why these events happened to them.

Next, ask the Holy Spirit to reveal God's truth to you about yourself, your father, others and about God Himself. Jesus said that His sheep hear His voice, so trust that He will reveal His truth to you. Pray that God will break the power of Satan's lies and implant His truth in its place. Ask some mature Christian friends to pray with you about breaking away any evil spiritual consequences that may be lingering from your experiences with your father. Open your heart and ask the Holy Spirit to heal your orphan's heart.

STEP #3: Release the emotional energy that infects your father wounds.

There is always a large amount of emotional energy involved in father wounds. There is grief over what you did not receive or have with your father. There is anger over what your father did or did not do. There is hurt and pain about not being loved the way you needed to be loved or delighted in as you so wanted. There is sadness, resentment and guilt. This emotional energy must be released for the healing to take place. Often it is in the presence of loving friends that the emotions, anger and tears can be expressed and released.

Some people find it helpful to picture their father sitting in the room with them. They visualize him sitting in a chair, picturing in their mind that he is sitting there listening to them as they express their feelings and hurts. If needed, screaming and hollering at the chair can help a person to release some of the deep anger or rage. Don't be surprised if vocalizing of the anger turns into crying and grief after you have released a lot of the negative emotions.

This emotional energy must be released for the healing to take place. Often it is before God in the presence of loving friends that the emotions, anger and tears can be released. Sometimes in your private prayer time you can release some of these feelings, but the best place is in the context of loving Christian friends who can witness your pain and offer you God's insights and comfort.

An assignment counselors often give a person is to write a very honest open letter to his or her father. Be very blunt about the specifics of the event and the related pain of the event. Let the emotions flow into the letter and do not censor your feelings or words. Just write it all down on paper even if it takes forty-two pages. DO NOT MAIL THE LETTER! Take it back to the person who gave you the assignment (or to another mature Christian) and read it out loud to that person as if your father was there in the room with the two of you listening to your feelings. This is similar to what King David did in the Psalms. When you read some of David's Psalms you recognize that he was venting his feelings about different events.

It is always good to let your feelings out with a caring loving person or to God in writing, but do not go and unload on the person who wounded you. It will only cause greater harm and it is not a Biblical strategy for healing (Read Romans 12:17-21).

STEP #4: Accept the reality that your father can never be what you wished him to be. Let go of the false hope.

Your father cannot give you what he does not have or did not have when you were a child. You can't go back and be his little girl or his favored son again. Time has passed; you are no longer a child.

Fathers usually do the best they can do with what they have emotionally. Often it is out of their own woundedness that they neglect, abuse and hurt their children. Most fathers do not set out to deliberately hurt their children. They, like you, parent the way they were parented and often do not realize how their own wounds are infecting the relationships with their children.

Release yourself from the false hope that someday, in someway, if you behave in just the exact right manner, you will get your father's love. Forgive your father and let your imagination rest.

Turn him over to God for God to deal with. Read Romans 12: 17-21 and give up any desire for revenge. Let God deal with your father because God is the only one who really knows the motives of his heart and the only one who can deal with him with justice and mercy.

STEP #5: Forgive your father as God has forgiven you.

It is important that you forgive your father and anyone else that has wounded you. Holding bitterness in your heart is the same as drinking poison hoping that the other person will die. Unforgiveness and bitterness destroy your immune system and make you vulnerable to all sorts of diseases and internal physical problems.

> *"Forgiveness is a choice, an act of your free will. It enables you to release all those toxic thoughts of anger, resentment, bitterness, shame, grief, regret, guilt and hate. These emotions hold your mind in a nasty, vice-like grip. Most importantly, as long as these unhealthy toxic thoughts dominate your mind, you will not be able to grow new healthy thoughts and memories."*
> Dr. Caroline Leaf, Who Switched off My Brain?

A study on forgiveness by researchers at the University of Wisconsin found that those who are able to forgive are significantly less angry, upset, and hurt. Consequently their immune systems are stronger and they are healthier.

But forgiveness is more than just praying to God and saying *"I forgive him."* Remember what Jesus did for your forgiveness. He took all of your sins and bore them on the Cross. He gave you His righteousness. This is what makes it possible for you and anyone else to have a relationship with God. This is what makes your forgiveness real.

You have to take your father to the Cross and see his sins laid on Jesus, too. Just like you, your father can only know forgiveness because he puts his trust in Jesus' atonement. If you have released your emotional energy, the grief and anger and rage about your father wounds and you have taken your father to the Cross, you can truly forgive him. Turn your father over to God for Him to deal with as He sees fit.

Forgiveness requires both a cognitive release and an emotional release; a lot of people have forgiven from their mind but their heart is still filled with bitterness. Let the bitterness go and let God deal with your father.

STEP #6: Find new healthy sources for masculine energy in your life.

Cultivate healthy relationships with healthy men…men who can mentor you like a surrogate father. These healthy men can help re-parent you and provide the healthy masculine energy you need for emotional healing. Husbands can provide some of this masculine energy for women, but they do not make the best resource because of the confusion that results when parenting components are mixed with sexual feelings in the relationship. Surrogate fathering relationships are always non-erotic relationships and, if they become sexual, they cease being healing.

God intended for the Church to be His family on earth, a healthy functional family. Unfortunately it has not always been that; many people have been disappointed or hurt in this family. But the Church can be a safe place if a person carefully selects those to be close to. Many times a small group setting will work well. The goal is to find healthy men and women who can serve as mentors, coaches or surrogate parents for those who have been wounded.

Men do best in a gender specific group with other men who offer unconditional love and acceptance in an atmosphere of transparency and vulnerability. Individual counseling or group counseling with a healthy male counselor also works for men and women. Another effective method is a small group of women led by a male counselor. The group setting enables the women to feel safer than in individual one-on-one counseling.

The goal is to cultivate healthy relationships with healthy men within the Church, the Body of Christ. God will use these healthy men to re-parent you and provide the healthy masculine energy you need for emotional healing. Paul used a similar strategy in his discipleship program at Thessalonica and likely in other cities as well.

Paul said in I Thessalonians 2:7: *"...We were gentle among you, like a mother caring for her little children."* Then in verses 11 & 12 he wrote: *"We dealt with each of you as a father deals with his own children, encouraging, comforting and urging you to live lives worthy of God..."* The entire relationship was because of Paul's love for the people: *"We loved you so much that we were delighted to share with you not only the gospel of God but our lives as well, because you had become so dear to us."*

Spiritual fathers are needed in the Church today. Older men who can mentor and coach are in great demand. A male pastor, coach or counselor can be an effective tool God can use for healing when the husband is aware of the relationship and the relationship is loving, totally safe and always non-erotic. The reality is that humans live in a two gender world by God's design. We need non-erotic relationships with both genders to be healthy.

STEP #7: Forgive yourself for the mistakes you made.

You tried to find a way to get your fathering needs met. You entered into relationships hoping for some comfort and healing, only to find that you picked an unsafe person or that you jumped too quickly into sexual activities or that you became too dependent on that person. Whatever mistakes you made, you must let go and forgive yourself. You were doing the best you could do at that time in your life. Self-condemnation and shame will only hinder your growth and healing. Let go of your need to punish yourself and forgive yourself for the mistakes you made.

We can forgive ourselves because we know that Jesus has forgiven us. In Romans 8:1, it says that there is no condemnation for those of us who are in Christ Jesus because when we confess our sins He forgives us and purifies us from all unrighteousness (I John 1:7,9). In II Corinthians 5:21, Paul wrote that Jesus took all our sins and gave us in exchange His righteousness. Now that was a good deal!

STEP #8: Make amends with your earthly father **if possible. At times, it might not be healthy or safe for you to make amends in person.**

During Father's Day week this past year, a fifty year old man approached me and told me about the letter he had received from his twenty-five year old son. He told me that he and his son had been estranged for years and that in this letter his son told him he forgave him for all that he, the father, had done. With tears streaming down his face, he recounted the joy this letter brought him.

Earlier that same week, another man, a seventy-three year old father, told me over breakfast about his family situation. His eyes were filled with tears. He said, *"I have been divorced for fourteen years and my children have never been to my home in all those years..."* He paused...then continued. *"But they are coming over this Father's Day weekend."*

The way to begin an amends process is to write out what you want to say to your father if you could be face-to-face with him. If you have not released the anger when you did Step # 3, then you will find the letter filled with angry words. Don't be surprised if a few tears drop on the page.

Once you have written out what you want to say, decide on the best way to present those words to your father. Be courageous and bold. Don't let your fears intimidate you. Ask God to give you the courage to talk to your earthly father.

A face-to-face conversation is always preferable, but not always possible.

For some of you there may be good reasons to not try to be in contact with your Dad. If you have reason to believe that your father might be dangerous, severely addicted or just real mean, then you might consider making contact with other family members to discern how safe you would be to be back in contact with him. If the abuse you experienced was life threatening or if you have reason to believe that he could be a threat to you, or if the trauma of your experiences with him are still overwhelming, then talk with your pastor or counselor about the decision. The goal of this step is healing, not further abuse.

So with the help of the prayers of Christian friends, make the decision: face-to-face, telephone, letter, or email. Make the move and tell your father that you forgive him. Perhaps there are things for which you need to ask him to forgive you. Do so. Remember the goal, when appropriate, is to eventually meet face-to-face and find a new connection with your Daddy.

What if your father is deceased? Some individuals go to the cemetery and sit by their father's grave. If not possible, write him a letter. When you finish the letter burn it or tear it up. Let God see that it gets delivered.

STEP #9: Allow God to transform you spiritually.

Recognize that your image of God is in need of healing and ask God to reveal to you who He really is.

Father wounds hinder your spiritual experiences because your God-image is often contaminated by your father wounds. For the healing process to continue, you will need to work toward a better understanding of your relationship with God, your Heavenly Father. The reality is that God is not like your earthly Father. God is good all the time. He is always there and He never deserts us or leaves us. He is forgiving and loving. As you continue to work through the first eight steps you will see that your God image is growing and changing. Marc Owens & David Terry wrote in The Original Sanctuary:

> *"He created a space, a vacuum, a blank spot in my heart and emotions that can only be filled by Him. The place is shaped like His presence. I am made in His image. His finger prints are smeared all over my body, soul and spirit. My need for safety and security can only be met by the Father. I need to hear His heartbeat."*

STEP #10: Seek healthy professional counseling if you are stuck or overwhelmed by the process.

Be wise and proactive when you choose a counselor or therapist. Ask friends for recommendations. Narrow the field and then make a "screening" interview appointment. Do you get a good sense of warmth and competence? Ask them specific questions about their experience with your type of issues. Ask them about their spiritual understanding of the issues.

Often a male therapist can more effectively enable you to access your father deprivation wounds and feelings better than a female therapist simply because your primary wound is from the masculine father. If the wound is a secondary wound by the mother, then a female therapist might be the most helpful. The critical ingredient is how safe you feel with the person.

STEP #11: If possible, talk with members of your family of origin. Share what you have learned.

It is not possible for everyone to take this step. In some cases, family members may be deceased or the issues within your family of origin could be too painful or fearful for you to consider such a conversation. However, there are times when a conversation and even a confrontation might be beneficial for your healing and freedom.

Some family structures are so dysfunctional with multiple divorces, step-parents, etc. that the only way you can understand the emotional wounds is through a detailed strategy with a counselor. If you are stuck, not knowing how to deal with a fearful family situation, talking with a counselor is appropriate.

STEP #12: Commit to be a healthier father or parent than you experienced as a child.

Most people parent the way they were parented unless they make an intentional effort to be different. One of the most important things you can do for your children is to seek healing for your own father deprivation wounds. Remember the way you parent imprints your child's heart and soul and dramatically affects their quality of life and relationships as adults. Find some resources and learn how to improve your parenting. The books and organizations listed at the back of this book should help.

These twelve steps are truly an introduction to your healing.

Remember the healing process is progressive and not a quick microwave experience. Allow God to progressively work in you to transform you and heal you through His process of spiritual growth.

Transformational healing is a process that continues all the rest of our lives. As we grow, the pain is healed and we experience more and more joy. We begin to understand more what God is doing in our lives and we learn that He is using our deepest woundedness to help other people.

Paul wrote in II Corinthians 1:3-4:

"Praise be to God and Father of our Lord Jesus Christ, the father of compassion and the God of all comfort, who comforts us in all our troubles, so that we can comfort those in any trouble with the comfort we ourselves have received from God."

Draw close to God through Jesus Christ and let His Spirit transform you day by day. You have a Father in Heaven who will never leave you nor forsake you (Hebrews 13:5). Let God be a loving father to you...your ABBA! (Romans 8:15-16; Galatians 4:6-7).

STEP #13: Commit to be pro-father. Work with corporations, businesses, schools and churches to encourage them to become pro-father resource centers in our society.

Today is the time for a major move among men and women toward changing the atmosphere in our culture about fathering. There is so much to be done. The only way anything gets changed in our society is when people get challenged and organized to address the issues. Our culture has a desperate need for a pro-father agenda. The issue of father deprivation will not change until someone steps up and says "Enough!"

STEP #14: Contact the following groups and ask to be added to their mailing lists and email notices.
National Fatherhood Initiative
101 Lake Forest Blvd. #360
Gaithersburg, MD 20877
www.fatherhood.org or call 301-948-0599

The National Center for Fathering
P.O. Box 413888— Kansas City, MO 64141
www.fathers.com or call 800-593-DADS

The Global Fathering Initiative
4003 Southwood Dr. West
Colleyville, TX 76034
www.globalfathering.com or waylon@globalfathering.com or
call 817-995-8318

Our society is made up of people desperately seeking what they were deprived of. Individuals with father wounds number in the millions, each one suffering in his/her own unique way from father deprivation. All looking for Daddy.

We have reported the research on father deprivation, both in our culture and globally. We have detailed the consequences for men, women and families. We have proposed a strategy for healing these wounds for you personally. We have suggested ideas on how you can become a healthy father advocate and share your healing with others.

The question is no longer whether or not we have a father deprivation problem. The question is, "What, if anything, are you willing and prepared to do about it?" Passivity in the face of the fathering crisis around the globe is indefensible.

CHAPTER ELEVEN

Some Final Thoughts

Healing the Father Wound is important for each individual. When we carry a father wound, it contaminates so much of our lives. Too often we think that it doesn't really matter what happened to us in our childhood experiences, but it does. Our unhealed wounds create vulnerabilities in our lives and our relationships. Here are a few of the ways that these wounds impact us.

- Wounded people wound other people. When we have a wound, it causes us to react to others out of our woundedness instead of out of Christian love. Those closest to us are the ones who are hurt the most.
- We parent the way we were parented unless we make a concerted effort to find healing of these wounds. Our children experience our woundedness and we pass it on to the next generation.
- We live from an orphan heart instead of from the heart of a son or daughter of God. The orphan heart underlies all of our

fears and causes us to distrust others. We are always reacting from our fears instead of from the awareness that we are deeply loved. The orphan never really feels safe and secure anywhere.

- We relate to God as a servant instead of a son or daughter. We are always trying to please God instead of living from the position of one who is delighted in by our Father.
- We have difficulty believing anyone can love us. We are always trying to get someone to love us, notice us, show us how important we are to them. We become too dependent on others for our worth and value.
- We never feel at home in our own skin. We live as if we have no home, no safe place to ever relax and be truly "at home." We struggle to find security and safety and peace because we are never sure what we have will last.

When our Father Wound is healed, we can experience the love of our Heavenly Father and feel the embrace of the Father and know that we are deeply loved. Our true home is in God our Father. Remember the younger son returning home to his father in Luke 15. Remember how the Father reacted:

"But while he was still a long way off, his father saw him. He ran to his son, threw his arms around him and kissed him."
Luke 15:20

Can you imagine your Father in Heaven doing this for you? God delights in you and He wants to make His home in you and your home in Him. You are His precious child.

"How great is the love the Father has lavished on us, that we should be called the children of God! And that is what we are!"
I John 3:1

There is no fear in love. But perfect love drives out fear, because fear has to do with punishment. The man who fears is not made perfect in love."

I John 4:18

"For you did not receive a spirit that makes you a slave again to fear, but you received the Spirit who makes you sons. And by Him we cry, 'Abba, Father.' The Spirit Himself testifies with our spirit that we are God's children."

Romans 8:15-16

Your home is with God. He is your Daddy, your Abba. He is waiting for you to come home so He can embrace you with His Father love.

"Do not let your hearts be troubled. Trust in God, trust also in me. There are many rooms in my Father's house; otherwise I would have told you. I am going to prepare a place for you. And if I go and prepare a place for you, I will come back and take you to be with me that you also may be where I am."

John 14:1-3

Come home where you belong. "Coming home" for me meant walking step by step toward the One who awaits me with open arms and wants to hold me in an eternal embrace, to intentionally walk one step at a time toward the One who is calling me home. As we learn to practice His presence with us and in us, we grow in our awareness of His loving acceptance and the healing of our wounds. We are transformed and healed by the love of our Father's embrace.

The Spirit of God draws us through our study of the Scriptures and through loving fellowship with others who are coming to know the Father's embrace. We learn to recognize His voice above the chaotic voices of our culture. We choose to walk in agreement with Him and take one step at a time, always trusting the outcome into His hands. We learn to trust His heart's embrace...we learn to relax in His arms. He is our Daddy.

So come home where you belong…to the loving embrace of the Father's Love.

Sources and Suggested Reading

Fatherless America
by David Blankenhorn

Save the Males
by Kathleen Parker

The War against Boys
by Christina Hoff Sommers

Faith of the Fatherless
by Paul C. Vitz

The Role of the Father in Child Development
edited by Michael E. Lamb

FATHER FACTS
edited and published by the National Fatherhood Initiative

The Search for Lost Fathering
by James L. Schaller

Crisis in Masculinity
by Leanne Payne

Healing of Damaged Emotions
by David Seamands

<u>Wild at Heart</u>
by John Eldredge

<u>Waking the Dead</u>
by John Eldredge

<u>Iron John</u>
by Robert Bly

<u>Spiritual Slavery to Spiritual Sonship</u>
by Jack Frost

<u>Experiencing Father's Embrace</u>
by Jack Frost

<u>Orphans At Home</u>
by Joe White

<u>Into Abba's Arms</u>
by Sandra D. Wilson

<u>Abba's Child</u>
by Brennen Manning

<u>The Return of the Prodigal</u>
by Henri Nouwen

<u>The Inner Voice of Love</u>
by Henri Nouwen

<u>Agape Road</u>
by Bob Mumford

<u>Healing the Father Wound</u>
by H. Norman Wright

Men In their Own Skin
by Dudley Hall

Who Switched Off My Brain
by Dr. Caroline Leaf

The Original Sanctuary
by Marc Owens & David Terry

GLOBAL FATHERING INITIATIVE
"Transforming a Fatherless World"

⚮

VISION STATEMENT:
"Challenging Men to Impact the World through Fathering."

MISSION STATEMENT:

1. *To restore Father Love and Fathering to the center of the Christian faith.*
2. *To honor and encourage spiritual fathers.*
3. *To facilitate seminars and conferences for the healing of father wounds.*
4. *To implement strategies to train and encourage men who are actively engaged in fathering.*
5. *To implement a pro-father strategy to be used in corporations, businesses and churches to enable these organizations to become pro-father resources.*
6. *To implement a strategy to establish and encourage men to be involved in surrogate fathering.*

FATHER LOVE IS THE HEART OF THE CHRISTIAN FAITH. Restoring Father Love to the center of the Church's mission to the world is a priority. Human fathers are pictures of the Heavenly Father. If these fathers do not accurately picture God the Father or if they are disconnected and not involved, then the next generation loses. And if the earthly father is irrelevant, how long will it be before the Heavenly Father will be irrelevant? An emphasis on healthy fathering is a major factor in the church's ability to successfully accomplish intergenerational transfer of the faith to younger generations.

The passion of GFI is to honor God the Father by healing father wounds, putting healthy fathers back in the home and restoring the noble role of the earthly father.

About Waylon Ward

⊙══╪══⊙

Waylon Ward graduated from Texas A& M University with a Bachelor of Arts Degree in English and History. He holds the Master of Arts Degree in Biblical Studies from Dallas Theological Seminary and a Master of Education Degree with an emphasis on Marriage and Family Counseling from Texas A&M Commerce.

After a ministry of six years with Campus Crusade for Christ, Waylon began Dallas Christian Counseling Services in 1975. It was the first distinctively Christian counseling ministry in the Dallas area and grew to be the largest such ministry in the Metroplex during the ten years that Waylon was the Director.

He is the author of The Bible in Counseling, published by Moody Press and His Image, My Image, published by Thomas Nelson, which he co-wrote with Josh McDowell. Sex Matters: Men Winning the Battle was published in 2004. He also wrote the group manual, M3: MEN MENTORING MEN.

Waylon is the author of the newspaper columns "Dad's World" and "DAD 2.0" which have appeared in many small town newspapers. In addition, he has written numerous articles in publications such as Moody Monthly, Kindred Spirit, Family Life Today, and Marriage Magazine. A popular speaker and seminar leader, Waylon has spoken on college campuses and churches in fifteen states and has conducted workshops and conferences throughout Texas. His main areas of emphasis include Men's Issues, Relationship Issues, Father Deprivation, Anger Management, Sexual Issues and Marriage & Family Issues.

A life member of the Christian Association for Psychological Studies and member of the American Association of Christian Counselors, Waylon has 40 years experience in Christian counseling. He is a Christian counselor and Life Coach with offices in Addison and Colleyville. He has more than 50,000 hours of counseling experience.

Waylon lives with his wife, Lynn, in Colleyville, Texas. They are the parents of six children and proud grandparents of eight. Waylon is the Executive Director of *MERCY MATTERS* and GLOBAL FATHERING INITIATIVE. He can be contacted at 214-415-3486 or email: waylon@mercymatters.com.

Sex Matters: Men Winning the Battle

- Presents a strategy designed to change the way men think about sex.
- Forged in the lives of ordinary Christian men who discovered an extraordinary power that enables them to walk in purity.
- Drawn from years of counseling experience and from his own personal journey, the author provides a practical spiritual strategy.

God wants to invade this secret war zone and bring healing and freedom.

available at mercymatters.com

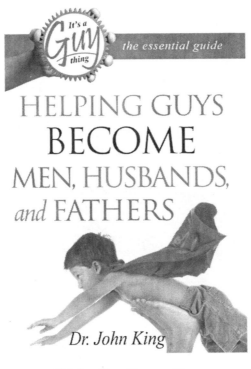

**Helping Guys Become Men,
Husbands, and Fathers**
Dr. John A. King

It's a Guy Thing takes you on the journey of fatherhood. Dr. King shows you, in this book, the skills necessary to become a good father. He shows you what can happen when a father is absent or simply not active in a child's life. Being a male is a matter of birth. Being a man is a matter of choice. This book will help you make that choice.

Now to Next
Dr. John A. King

What does the next generation church look like? Who are the people that will be involved in the next generation church? How will it come about?

Those are some of the questions answered in Dr. King's newest release, *Now to Next: Blueprint for a Christian Revolution.*

INTERNATIONAL
MEN'S NETWORK

The International Men's Network was founded by Dr. John A. King. Its purpose is to help men grow to become the leaders their families and churches need and become men of God that make a lasting impact on those around them.

IMN is a missionary organization to the men of the world. We are committed to:

> • Inspire all men to rise to a high standard of biblical manhood.
> • Encourage them to excel in their roles as men, leaders, husbands, and
fathers.
> • Challenge them to be contributors to society and set an example based
> upon a biblical value system that will benefit this generation and lay a solid
> foundation for the next generation.

The International Men's Network is dedicated to providing and hosting the best resources for men, including teachings and lessons on CD and DVD and conferences that teach men the principles that will help them become more influential and effective in their lives.

For more information about IMN and its mission, visit us online at
www.imnonline.org or call 817.993.0047

Business By The Book
Dr. John A. King

The world's greatest handbook on leadership, economic and social excellence is not found in schoolbooks, but is Scripture. The principles in this book are tried, proven and resilient over centuries. Christ bet His life on it, and so can you.

Dear Daddy,

I missed you again tonight. As I sat by my window, wondering how my life would have been different if I had known you and you had known me...I missed you.

There were conversations we never had.
   There were hugs we never felt.
     There was fun we never shared.
      There was joy we never knew.
     There were questions I never asked,
   and feelings I never expressed.
  There was a man I never knew,
and a man you missed, too.

Daddy,
Where were you?
Where did you go so I could not find you?

I remember what you looked like,
    but I can't remember how your arms felt
   or how you smelled...
     or how your laugh sounded.

I remember the silence,
  the painful silence,
   that felt so lonely, so empty, so scary.

Daddy, where did you go?
I missed you again tonight.
        April 5, 1990

164